NEGOTIATING STRATEGIES

[
REWARDING, EDUCATIONAL, PROFESSIONAL
]

JAMES A. SMITH

authorHOUSE®

AuthorHouse™
1663 Liberty Drive
Bloomington, IN 47403
www.authorhouse.com
Phone: 1 (800) 839-8640

Published by AuthorHouse   06/03/2015

ISBN: 978-1-5049-1422-2 (sc)
ISBN: 978-1-5049-1421-5 (e)

Library of Congress Control Number: 2015908250

Print information available on the last page.

FOREWORD

Each year, millions of Americans seek a pay raise – or adjustment in salary – from respective employers. Approximately one-half of these employees are disappointed with the outcome. A substantial number of the "rejected" will seek employment elsewhere, only to find the same critical rejection criteria on the part of a new employer.

What is an employee to do? Well let's begin by a thorough review of the material in this book. You will find many sections and/or chapters applicable to those who are actively seeking a salary adjustment.

But why are we concentrating our attention on salaries? After all, this book is designed to facilitate negotiating at various levels by many people. Some examples for your consideration:

- Husband and wife, or vice versa
- Parents and children, and parent-teacher
- Negotiating the purchase of a new home, auto or other applicable item
- Achieve improved working relations between co-workers
- And the list goes on, and is almost endless

THANKS

A special tribute to Mary Portwood Artley whose support was truly indispensable during the creation of this book. Her demonstrated efficiency will prove invaluable in future manuscripts.

Contents

A NEGOTIATION IS SIMPLY AN AGREEMENT BETWEEN TWO OR MORE PARTIES, WITH ALL PARTIES HAVING THE RIGHT TO VETO

FOREWORD

NEGOTIATING IS A LEARNED EXPERIENCE. FACT IS, YOU ARE NOT BORN WITH THE SKILLS REQUIRED TO BE AN EFFECTIVE NEGOTIATOR. WHAT YOU DO NEED IS A DESIRE TO LEARN NEGOTIATING TECHNIQUES, WHICH CAN COME FROM WRITTEN INFORMATION OR EXPOSURE TO MORE SKILLED NEGOTIATORS. OBVIOUSLY, THIS BOOK WILL BE VERY IMPORTANT IN YOUR SEARCH FOR KNOWLEDGE.

ALLOW ME TO EMPHASIZE A FEW IMPORTANT TOPICS FOR THE READER. LET'S BEGIN WITH RESEARCH. YOUR LEVEL OF NEGOTIATING KNOWLEDGE WILL INCREASE AS YOU RESEARCH PERTINENT TOPICS.

NEXT, UNDERSTAND THAT YOU HAVE OPTIONS IN NEGOTIATING WITH OTHERS. LOOK FOR THEM!

EARLY ON IN A NEGOTIATING SESSION, DETERMINE YOUR OPPONENT'S INTEREST AND PLANS. ASK THE QUESTION – WHAT DO YOU SEEK IN THIS NEGOTIATION? SET GROUND RULES IN THE BEGINNING.

AS YOUR NEGOTIATING SESSION GETS UNDERWAY, DON'T BE RELUCTANT TO CHANGE SOMETHING IF THE SESSION IS BOGGED DOWN. THE SETTING OR VENUE CAN OFTEN BE INFLUENCED BY THE OUTCOME.

CHAPTER ONE

LEARNING HIGHLIGHTS – KEY POINTS

- **A FEW KEY IMPORTANT HIGHLIGHTS FROM THESE SESSIONS ARE DETAILED BELOW. THESE GO HAND-IN-HAND WITH ALL OTHER ASPECTS TO:**

  - MEASURABLY INCREASE YOUR KNOWLEDGE OF NEGOTIATING STRATEGIES

  - BETTER PREPARE YOU FOR THE "TIGERS" THAT WILL CONFRONT YOU ACROSS THE TABLE. THESE "MANEATERS," SO TO SPEAK, TAKE NO PRISONERS!! THEY ARE NOT YOUR FRIENDS. GIVE THEM REASON TO RESPECT YOUR KNOWLEDGE AND DETERMINATION AND WINNABILITY.

- **THE POPULAR TERM, "WIN-WIN" CAN BE HARMFUL. STATED ANOTHER WAY, THE TERM EQUALS "COMPROMISE."**

  - COMPROMISE CANNOT BE GOOD, BECAUSE YOU ARE LIKELY GIVING UP SOMETHING

  - THE ECONOMIC HEALTH OF ANY COMPANY IS IN NO SMALL PART RELATED TO BUYER PERFORMANCE AND KNOWLEDGE, AND WILLINGNESS TO BECOME "INUNDATED" IN THE MANY TECHNIQUES CONTAINED HEREIN. COMPROMISE IS ONE KEY WAY TO DENY ECONOMIC HEALTH, AS YOU WILL SEE

- **THE "TIGER" ACROSS THE TABLE HAS SHARP TEETH AND A MASSIVE APPETITE. HE/SHE IS, IN FACT, YOUR ADVERSARY . . . NEVER YOUR FRIEND.**
  - YOU CAN CALL HIM/HER YOUR "RESPECTED OPPONENT" IF ADVERSARY BOTHERS YOU

- **ALMOST ALL NEGOTIATING DECISIONS ARE EMOTION-BASED, NOT DECISION-BASED. EMOTIONALLY-BASED NEGOTIATING PLAYS ON YOUR HEART STRINGS**
  - KEEP YOUR EYE FOCUSED ON THE OBJECTIVE, NOT WHETHER YOU WIN

- **SUCCESS SOMETIMES MEANS WALKING AWAY WITH A POLITE "GOODBYE." THESE SESSIONS WILL HELP YOU.**

- **YOUR ADVERSARY USES A DEVICE WITH A HIGH-POWER TELESCOPIC LENS – YOU ARE THE TARGET**

- **UNDERSTAND THE GREATEST WEAKNESS OF ALL – NEEDINESS**
  - THE MOMENT YOU EXPRESS NEED, YOU'VE LOST CONTROL

  - TIGERS ARE EXPERTS IN RECOGNIZING NEED – AND IN CREATING NEED

- **ALSO NOTE THAT "YES" AND "MAYBE" ARE INCONCLUSIVE**
    - THE JAPANESE WILL DRIVE YOU CRAZY WITH "MAYBE" – WHAT DOES IT REALLY MEAN? TIE IT DOWN!!

- **SAYING "NO" SHOULD NOT BOTHER YOU – IT CLEARLY DEFINES YOUR POSITION**

- **MANY NEGOTIATORS WANT TO BE LIKED – IT WILL LEAD TO TROUBLE FOR YOU!!**
    - DON'T SAVE THE ADVERSARY OR SAVE THE RELATIONSHIP. DON'T FEAR HURTING FEELINGS

- **GET INFORMATION BY ASKING QUESTIONS – DO NOT GIVE INFORMATION IF IT CAN BE AVOIDED.**

CHAPTER TWO

NINE WAYS TO CALM AND MELLOW

- **TRY NOT TO ACT LIKE YOU ATE A LEMON FOR BREAKFAST**
    - SMILING IS A CHEAP CONCESSION – LOWERS ADVERSARY'S SHIELD

    - WHEN PLEASANT AND POSITIVE, YOU ARE PERCEIVED AS CONFIDENT

- **USE FIRST NAME, ALWAYS**
    - PEOPLE LIKE TO BE CALLED BY THEIR FIRST NAME

    - FORMALITY MEANS ARM LENGTH NEGOTIATIONS

    - EASIER TO GAIN CONCESSIONS WHEN NOT VIEWED AS AN ADVERSARY

- **EASE INTO NEGOTIATIONS**
    - DISCUSS ANYTHING TO SET A PERSONAL TONE

    - BREAK THE ICE – HELP YOUR ADVERSARY RELAX

    - RELAX – TAKE YOUR TIME

- **BE OPTIMISTIC**
    - AT LEAST ACT LIKE YOU ARE

    - EXPRESSION OF OPTIMISM IS A GOOD TACTIC

- LET YOUR AUDIENCE VISUALIZE A SUCCESSFUL DEAL

- EARLY STAGE OPTIMISM GETS OTHER SIDE ENGAGED AND ENCOURAGES PARTICIPATION

- **USE CONFIDENCE – BUILDING GESTURES (NOT CONCESSIONS)**
  - SHOW INTEREST IN CONCERNS AND FEARS OF OTHERS

  - SHOW WILLINGNESS TO ACHIEVE AN AGREEMENT

- **SEARCH FOR COMMON GROUND**
  - COMMON VALUES – RELIGION, POLITICS, SOCIAL

  - COMMON PROBLEMS – COST OF NEGOTIATIONS, SUCH AS ATTORNEY FEES

- **STATE ADVERSARY'S POSITION BETTER THAN THEY DO – EVEN IF YOU DISAGREE – DO YOUR RESEARCH!!**
  - PERMITS YOU TO BETTER SEE THE PROBLEMS – ALLOWS YOU TO ADDRESS REAL CONCERNS

  - ADVERSARIES MORE LIKELY TO LISTEN TO YOUR VIEWPOINT WHEN THEY BELIEVE YOU UNDERSTAND THEIR POSITION

- **PROMOTE PRIVACY**
  - RESOLVE DISPUTES PRIVATELY AND AWAY FROM OTHER EARS

  - SEEK A QUIET ROOM FOR DISCUSSION

- DO NOT TALK ABOUT YOUR NEGOTIATIONS – KEEP THEM PRIVATE

- RESOLVE PROBLEMS QUICKLY

- **HELP ADVERSARY SAVE FACE**
  - WHEN WE LOSE FACE, WE RETALIATE

  - NEVER POINT OUT THEY BACKED OFF A POSITION – UNLESS YOU HAVE TO

  - GET ADVERSARY A WAY OUT OF THEIR DILEMMA – GIVE A BRIDGE TO RETREAT

  - LOOK FOR WAYS YOUR ADVERSARY CAN SELL THE DEAL TO OTHERS WHO MAY BE IN THE APPROVAL CHAIN

NOTE: THESE VARIOUS POINTS ARE CRITICAL TO SUCCESSFUL NEGOTIATING. HOWEVER, DON'T ALLOW THIS TO LOCK YOU INTO A FORCED "WIN-WIN" NEGOTIATING SESSION. REMEMBER – "WIN-WIN" MEANS SOMEONE . . . . .

CHAPTER THREE

NEGOTIATING STYLES

- **THE BULLDOG**
    - AGGRESSIVE, DOMINEERING STYLE
    - NEGOTIATING VIEWED AS A BATTLE OF WILLS
    - WINNING IS MORE IMPORTANT THAN THE DEAL
    - THEY USE DEMANDS, EXTORTION TO WIN
    - CONCESSIONS ARE MADE GRUDGINGLY, IF AT ALL

- **DEALING WITH THE BULLDOG**
    - QUESTION THE BASIS OF HIS/HER POSITIONS
    - DON'T NECESSARILY RESPOND TO THEIR OUTRAGEOUS DEMANDS
    - DON'T STAND FOR AGGRESSIVE BEHAVIOR
    - IF YOU ARE ATTACKED PERSONALLY, PROMPTLY RESPOND BY CHALLENGING THEIR POSITION. **"LETS KEEP BAD FEELINGS OUT OF THIS"**
    - DON'T FALL VICTIM TO PUTDOWNS OR INSULTS
    - A CRUSHING HANDSHAKE SHOULD ALERT YOU TO EXPECT THE BULLDOG TREATMENT
    - YOU MAY BE FORCED TO SAY, **"IT LOOKS LIKE WE JUST CAN'T DO BUSINESS TOGETHER . . . MAYBE NEXT TIME"**

- **THE FOX**
    - OPERATES FROM A SECRETIVE, MANIPULATIVE MINDSET
    - THEY FORCE YOU TO GUESS THEIR MOTIVATIONS AND INTENTIONS

- THEY RELY ON AMBIGUITY AND SUBTERFUGE TO GET WHAT THEY WANT
- OPPONENTS FEEL LIKE THEY CAN'T TRUST THEM
  - NOTE: THE FOX COULD BE MORE APPEALING TO THE WELL-EDUCATED OR INTELLECTUALLY-ORIENTED

- **DEALING WITH THE FOX**
  - YOUR BEST TOOL IS <u>INFORMATION</u>. THE MORE YOU KNOW, THE MORE YOU CAN NEUTRALIZE ATTEMPTS AT TRICKERY OR DECEIT
  - FOCUS ON INTERESTS, VALUES, OPTIONS
  - SEARCH FOR THE FOX'S HIDDEN AGENDA
  - ENCOURAGE MORE OPENNESS AND COMPLIANCE BY MODELING IT YOURSELF

- **THE DEER**
  - THEY LIKELY WILL BOLT IF THEY GET INTO A THREATENING SITUATION THAT REMOVES THEM FROM THEIR COMFORT ZONE
  - THEY TEND TO BE PASSIVE, ACCOMMODATING, WITHOUT MAKING WAVES OR ANTAGONIZING ANYONE
  - THEY FEAR CONFLICT OR CONFRONTATION
  - THEY USUALLY WORK BY EVASION OR APPEASEMENT, SO AS NOT TO UPSET ANYONE
  - THEY ALLOW THE OTHER PARTY TO DICTATE AND CONTROL THE PROCESS, AND ACQUIESCE TO OTHER SIDE'S PROPOSALS
  - NOTE (1) MANY PEOPLE IN THIS CATEGORY CHEAT THEMSELVES AND LEAVE TOO MUCH ON THE TABLE
  - NOTE (2) THE DEER DESCRIBES THE MAJORITY OF THE ADULT-NEGOTIATING POPULATION. THIS

PERSON WILL BE VERY RELUCTANT TO DO BATTLE WITH THE PUSHY CAR SALESPERSON
- NOTE (3) THE AGGRESSIVE BEHAVIOR OF THE BULLDOG AND FOX TENDS TO CAUSE THE DEER TO CAPITULATE AND ACCEPT INFERIOR DEALS
- NOTE (4) PEOPLE WITH DEER CHARACTERISTICS TEND TO REGRESS TO THE FOX OR BULLDOG WHEN THEY FEEL INSECURE OR THREATENED BY EITHER OF THE OTHER TWO STYLES

- ## DEALING WITH THE DEER
  - USUALLY EASIEST TO DEAL WITH – NOT AGGRESSIVE
  - CREATE COMFORT ZONE FOR THIS PERSON – IMPORTANT!
  - RESIST HIGH-PRESSURE TACTICS
    - FORCES THE DEER INTO A SHELL
    - DEER WILL FLEE THE SCENE
    - DEER IS UNCOMFORTABLE ABOUT MAKING A CRITICAL DECISION

  - ENSURE THE DEER KNOWS YOU ARE INTERESTED IN A GOOD DEAL – NOT IN WINNING THE NEGOTIATING WAR!

- ## THE PEACOCK
  - THEY SEEK TO BALANCE SELF-INTERESTS WITH THE INTERESTS OF OTHERS – A VERY UNUSUAL BIRD, INDEED!
  - THEY ARE FAIR, OPEN, HONEST, EMPATHETIC, COMPLIANT
  - THEY ARE MORE COMFORTABLE WITH AN ALL-WIN APPROACH IN NEGOTIATING

- THEY DON'T ENGAGE IN PERSONAL ATTACKS OR ARGUMENTS
- THEY BELIEVE IN OFFERING A RANGE OF ALTERNATIVES
- THEY LIKE TO SEE YOU DO WELL, BUT THEY WANT TO DO WELL ALSO
- THEIR INSTINCTS AND ABILITY WILL USUALLY RESULT IN A GOOD DEAL WITHOUT RESORTING TO PRACTICES OF THE BULLDOG OR FOX
- **"I'LL GET A BETTER DEAL FOR MYSELF BY GIVING THE OTHER PARTY A GOOD DEAL, TOO"**

- ## DEALING WITH THE PEACOCK
  - A RARE BIRD, INDEED!
  - THIS IS AN INFREQUENT FIND

CHAPTER FOUR

GENDER VARIATIONS – MEN VS. WOMEN

- **WOMEN ARE LESS LIKELY THAN MEN TO ENROLL IN TRAINING PROGRAMS ON NEGOTIATING**

- **MANY MEN SUBSCRIBE UNCONSCIOUSLY OR CONSCIOUSLY TO SO-CALLED WARRIOR VALUES IN BUSINESS**
  - METAPHORS USED BY MEN IN NEGOTIATING SESSIONS INCLUDE WARFARE, COMBAT, TACTICS, SPORT, CAPTURING TERRITORY
  - MALES ASSIGN LOWER VALUE TO SOCIAL CLIMATE, HUMAN NEEDS, CONFLICT AVOIDANCE THAN WOMEN DO

- **MOST WOMEN ARE NOT FULLY COMFORTABLE WITH WARFARE AS A FRAME OF REFERENCE**
  - MOST WOMEN ARE ALSO NOT ACCUSTOMED TO USING FIGURE OF SPEECH IN SPORTS IN EXPRESSING IDEAS

CHAPTER FIVE

MISSION AND PURPOSE

- **CORNERSTONE OF PREPARATION FOR ANY THOROUGH NEGOTIATION SESSION IS PREPARATION OF M&P STATEMENT**
    - SET IN ADVERSARY'S WORLD
        - CLEARLY AND WITHOUT FALSE ASSUMPTION
        - YOUR WORLD IS SECONDARY

        EXAMPLE: MY M&P HELPS PEOPLE IN THE LIGHTING INDUSTRY TO SEE, DISCOVER, DECIDE AND EXPERIENCE THE WORLD OF BRIGHTNESS, IMAGINATION AND POSSIBILITY RESULTING FROM CREATION OF ASTONISHING LEDs. WE DO THIS BY SHARING THE KNOWLEDGE OF OUR COMPANY IN A WAY THAT IS SUSTAINABLE NOW AND INTO THE FUTURE.

    - THE M&P DOES NOT "SELL 10,000 TOOLS" THE FIRST YEAR
    - INSTEAD, IT ALLOWS YOU TO ENTER YOUR ADVERSARY'S WORLD, HIS NEEDS, HOPES, PLANS IN A GENERAL MANNER
    - FOR MUTLI-FACETED COMPANIES, THE NEGOTIATOR MAY HAVE MORE THAN ONE M&P
    - YOUR M&P REQUIRES CONSTANT REFOCUSING

CHAPTER SIX

DECISION MAKING PRIOR TO NEGOTIATING

- **YOU HAVE A BETTER CHANCE OF ACTING RATIONALLY, NOT EMOTIONALLY, WHEN YOU MAKE DECISIONS PRIOR TO ENTERING THE NEGOTIATING ROOM**
  - WHAT ARE THE CONSEQUENCES OF A DEADLOCK?
  - WHAT IS THE COST OF A DEADLOCK TO ME?
  - WHAT ARE MY REAL UNDERLYING NEEDS?
  - WHAT JUSTIFICATION WILL I TAKE FOR THE POSITIONS I TAKE?
  - WHAT IS MY NEGOTIATING GOAL?
  - WHAT IS MY DEADLINE? IS CHANGE IN DEADLINE FEASIBLE?
  - WHAT ARE THE CONSEQUENCES OF FAILING TO MEET THEIR DEADLINE?

CHAPTER SEVEN

TEAM NEGOTIATIONS

- **ADVANTAGES**
  - MORE INFORMATION

  - MORE EXPLICIT

  - NUMBERS OVERWHELM THE OPPOSITION

- **DISADVANTAGES**
  - DISAGREEMENTS

  - DISRUPTIONS

  - GREATER DANGER FOR LEAKAGE OF INFORMATION

  - UNAUTHORIZED CONCESSIONS

  - THE LARGER THE TEAM, THE SLOWER THE RESPONSE

ORGANIZING THE TEAM

- **IDEAL TEAM IS COMPROMISED OF SEVEN DISTINCT ROLES:**
  - <u>CHIEF</u>: TOUGH BUT FRIENDLY. MOST IMPORTANT POSITION. THE ONLY BOSS.
    - SELECTS TEAM MEMBERS

    - PLANS OVERALL STRATEGY

- MAINTAINS CONTROL

- THINKS STRATEGICALLY

- LEADER, NOT AUTOCRAT

- LISTENER, NOT A TALKER

- SPOKESPERSON:
  - COMMUNICATES TEAM'S POSITION AND ATTITUDES

  - FLEXIBLE ETHICS

- TOUGH PERSON:
  - NOT AFRAID TO THREATEN THE OTHER SIDE

  - RESPONDS TO TOUGH PEOPLE

  - HAS A GENUINELY TOUGH IMAGE

  - BALANCED BY SELF-RESTRAINT

- FRIENDLY PERSON:
  - MAINTAINS CONTACT IF NEGOTIATIONS BREAK DOWN

  - GENUINELY FRIENDLY IMAGE

  - PERCEPTIVE AND TACTFUL

  - CAPABLE OF SELF-RESTRAINT

- TOLERATES PRESSURE FROM ONE'S OWN TEAM

- BEHAVIORAL ANALYST:
  - ANALYZES OTHER TEAM'S ACTIONS – UNDERSTANDS HOW OTHER SIDE REACTS

  - REPORT ANALYSIS TO THE CHIEF

  - UNDERSTANDS SUBTLE SIGNALS

  - COMFORTABLE – TAKES PASSIVE ROLE

  - THIS ROLE FILLED BY SOMEONE INFLUENTIAL AND PERCEPTIVE

- DATA ANALYST:
  - RECORD AND ANALYZE NUMBERS (NUMBER "CRUNCHER")

  - WORK WITH OTHER SIDE'S DATA ANALYST

  - HAS ORDERLY MIND, CALCULATES QUICKLY

  - POSSESSES COMMUNICATION SKILLS

  - COMFORTABLE WITH ASSIGNED ROLE

  - QUIET DURING NEGOTIATIONS

- SPECIALIST:
  - SUCH AS ATTORNEY, BUYER, ENGINEER, CONTRACT ADMINISTRATOR, ETC.

- BE EXPERT IN AREA BEING NEGOTIATED

- BE CREDIBLE WITH BOTH TEAMS

NOTES:

(1) **WHEN SHORT ON PERSONNEL, AVOID MIXING DISSIMILAR AREAS, SUCH AS "FRIENDLY" AND "TOUGH" PERSONS**

(2) **AGREE ON ALL TOPICS IN ADVANCE OF NEGOTIATING**

(3) **RESOLVE QUESTIONS AND DISAGREEMENTS PRIVATELY**

(4) **FORBID PRIVATE CONVERSATIONS WITH OTHER SIDE**

(5) **DEMAND THAT EVERYONE SUPPORT THE TEAM'S STRATEGY, OR LEAVE THE TEAM**

(6) **STAY IN YOUR ROLE**

CHAPTER EIGHT

PSYCHOLOGICAL BLOCKS TO NEGOTIATING

- **BE NICE**
  - NOBODY WANTS OPPONENT TO GO AWAY MAD
  - THE "POWER NEGOTIATOR" MAY STORM OUT OF THE ROOM WITH BRIEFCASE IN HAND SEEKING LARGER CONCESSION FROM YOU
  - THE NEED TO BE NICE COULD LEAD TO SMALLER SETTLEMENT TO AVOID TROUBLE
- **MOST NEGOTIATORS WANT TO BE ACCEPTED, TO FIT IN, TO RECEIVE STROKES, EVEN FROM OPPONENTS**
- **THE FEAR OF CONFRONTATION AT THE TABLE RAISES BLOOD PRESSURE FOR ALL**
- **POWER NEGOTIATORS KNOW HOW TO MAKE SOME PEOPLE FEEL UNCOMFORTABLE**
  - AGGRESSIVE
  - BULLYING
  - GUILT TRIPS – KEEPS TIMID DOWN
- **THE FEAR OF BEING "TAKEN" IS PREVALENT IN PEOPLE WHO HAVE BEEN THROUGH WIN-LOSE NEGOTIATIONS**
  - THEY WORRY ABOUT GETTING THE "SHAFT" WHICH MAKES IT NEARLY IMPOSSIBLE TO NEGOTIATE WITH THEM
- **DOMINEERING NEGOTIATORS INTIMIDATE OTHERS**

- SHY, RESERVED NEGOTIATORS CONFRONTED BY A BULLYING NEGOTIATOR ARE ALREADY BEHIND THE CURVE
- THE POWER NEGOTIATOR KNOWS WHICH BUTTON TO PUSH TO PUT THE SHY PERSON BACK IN HIS OR HER SHELL
- THE SHY PERSON WILL NOT GET THE BEST DEAL

- **LACK OF SELF-CONFIDENCE EQUALS LOW SELF-ESTEEM**
  - THE POWER NEGOTIATOR'S PLOYS UNDERMINE THE OPPONENT'S SENSE OF SELF-WORTH
  - SHY NEGOTIATOR TENDS TO GIVE AWAY CONCESSIONS JUST TO GET THE WHOLE EVENT OVER WITH

- **THINKING UNDER PRESSURE IS DIFFICULT**
  - POWER NEGOTIATORS WILL THROW MANY ISSUES AT THE OTHER PARTY
  - THE POWER NEGOTIATOR WILL ASK FOR A NUMBER OF IMMEDIATE CONCESSIONS, HOPING HE OR SHE WILL MAKE JUDGMENT ERRORS IN THE PROCESS

- **NEGOTIATOR'S REMORSE CAN SURFACE**
  - "DID I MAKE THE RIGHT DECISION?"
  - "DID I PAY TOO MUCH?"
  - "DID I GET A GOOD DEAL?"

- **FEAR OF LOSING FACE WITH BOSS OR COLLEAGUES COULD EXIST**
  - ADDED PRESSURE CAN MAKE THE TIMID NEGOTIATOR RELUCTANT TO ACT OR MAKE GOOD DECISIONS

- **LESSONS FOR THE "DISADVANTAGES" NEGOTIATOR**
  - SLOW THE ENTIRE PROCESS DOWN

- TAKE FREQUENT BREAKS TO "GET YOUR HEAD TOGETHER"
- CONSULT A TRUSTED COLLEAGUE
- IT MAY BE DIFFICULT – BUT STAND YOUR GROUND!! DON'T ALLOW THE POWER NEGOTIATOR TO OVERWHELM YOU – BECAUSE HE/SHE IS CAPABLE TO DOING SO!!

CHAPTER NINE

SOME QUESTIONS TO ASK
PRIOR TO NEGOTIATING

- WHAT <u>TOPICS</u> WILL BE DISCUSSED?
- WHAT IS <u>PURPOSE</u> OF THE NEGOTIATING SESSION?
- WHAT IS YOUR OPPONENT'S <u>PURPOSE</u> IN THIS SESSION?
- WHAT IS YOUR VISION OF THE PERFECT OUTCOME?
- FOR RESEARCH PURPOSES, WHAT IS YOUR SOURCE(S) OF RELEVANT INFORMATION?
- WILL YOU TALK WITH FRIENDS AND ASSOCIATES?
- WILL YOU NEGOTIATE WITH A TEAM, OR BY YOURSELF?
- WILL YOU SHOP THE COMPETITION?
- CAN YOU DETERMINE HOW YOUR OPPONENT IS COMPENSATED (MAY REVEAL LEVEL OF MOTIVATION)
- WHAT ARE THE VARIOUS ISSUES TO NEGOTIATE (PRICE, TERMS, QUALITY, WARRANTY, MODE OF SHIPMENT, ETC)
- WOULD A 3RD PARTY, SUCH AS A LAWYER, BE PRESENT?

CHAPTER TEN

BUILDING TRUST IN NEGOTIATING

- **WHEN IT COMES TO EARNING TRUST, ACTIONS SPEAK LOUDER THAN WORDS. MAKING YOUR OPPONENT TRUST YOU IS KEY TO SUCCESSFUL NEGOTIATING**
  - <u>DEMONSTRATE YOUR COMPETENCE</u> – WE ARE ALL MORE COMFORTABLE WITH SOMEONE WE CAN LOOK TO FOR HONEST ANSWERS, OPINIONS AND SOLUTIONS
  - NONVERBAL SIGNALS MUST MATCH WORDS YOU SAY. CONGRUENCE BETWEEN YOUR VERBAL AND NONVERBAL MESSAGES HELP CREATE TRUST
  - COMMUNICATE OUR GOOD INTENTIONS. MOST PEOPLE WILL GIVE GREATER LEEWAY IF THEY KNOW INTENTIONS ARE GOOD
  - MAINTAIN A PROFESSIONAL APPEARANCE. ENHANCE YOUR WELL-GROOMED APPEARANCE WITH GOOD POSTURE, CAREFUL CHOICE OF WORDS, CONFIDENT VOICE AND GOOD EYE-TO-EYE CONTACT
  - DO WHAT YOU SAY. KEEP YOUR PROMISES AND HONOR YOUR COMMITMENTS
  - GO BEYOND THE CONVENTIONAL RELATIONSHIP. WHAT "EXTRA" CAN YOU ADD TO THE RELATIONSHIP?
  - <u>LISTEN</u>. LISTEN OPENLY EVEN IF YOU DISAGREE WITH YOUR OPPONENT
  - <u>UNDER COMMUNICATE</u>. DON'T COMMUNICATE LESS WHEN THE GOING GETS TOUGH

- <u>DISCUSS THE UNDISCUSSED</u>. MANY ISSUES ARE DIFFICULT TO DISCUSS; SALARY IS AN EXAMPLE

- **IF YOU HAVE NO CHOICE ABOUT NEGOTIATING WITH A PARTICULAR OPPONENT THAT YOU DON'T TRUST, THE FOLLOWING SAFEGUARDS MAY PROVE HELPFUL**
  - ENSURE EVERY DEAL POINT IS MEASURABLE. SPELL OUT TERMS (IN WRITING)
  - ENSURE THAT EVERY DEAL POINT IS TIME BOUND; FOR EXAMPLE, WHEN WILL THE PRODUCT ARRIVE? OTHER ITEMS?
  - BUILD PENALTIES FOR NONPERFORMANCE INTO THE AGREEMENT. WHAT HAPPENS IF DELIVERY IS LATE? DOLLARS DEDUCTED?
  - WHAT IS YOUR OPPONENT'S MANUFACTURING CAPACITY? HAS THIS BEEN VERIFIED?
  - WHAT IF YOUR OPPONENT CANNOT MEET THE REQUESTED DELIVERY DATE? HAS OVERTIME BEEN RESORTED TO? WILL YOU PAY THE EXTRA EXPENSE? CONSIDER EVALUATING THEIR PROMPTNESS
  - HAS YOUR OPPONENT DEMONSTRATED WAYS OF CURTAILING COST? HOW SUCCESSFUL HAS HE BEEN? HOW DO YOU VERIFY HIS EFFECTIVENESS? ARE RECORDS MAINTAINED?
  - DOES YOUR OPPONENT REQUIRE A LARGE DOWN PAYMENT, EVEN THOUGH HIS CREDIT RATING MAY BE SECURE? IS HIS BUSINESS "SHAKY" AND HOW DO YOU VERIFY CURRENT STATUS? INCIDENTALLY, DOES YOUR OPPONENT HAVE DOCUMENTED EVIDENCE OF SUCCESS IN REDUCING COST OVER THE LAST THREE YEARS, OR DO YOU TRUST HIS STATEMENT IN THIS REGARD?

- CAN YOU TRUST YOUR OPPONENT TO MAKE DELIVERY IN A TIMELY MANNER? IF NOT, IS HE WILLING TO ACCEPT A PENALTY CLAUSE FOR LATE DELIVERY?
- CAN YOU TRUST CONCLUSIONS AND PROGRESS ON R&D, ESPECIALLY AS IT PERTAINS TO THE NEGOTIATION SESSION NOW UNDERWAY?
- IS YOUR OPPONENT FLEXIBLE ON PAYMENT TERMS? HOW CAN YOU TRUST HIS STATEMENTS ON THIS MATTER?
- YOUR OPPONENT HAS A SHORTER WARRANTY THAN HIS COMPETITORS BECAUSE HE CLAIMS HIS PRODUCT IS "SUPERIOR." WHAT IS YOUR RESPONSE?
- WILL YOUR OPPONENT AGREE ON A NEUTRAL THIRD PARTY TO RESOLVE ANY DISPUTES? WILL THEY AGREE ON MEDIATION OR ARBITRATION TO RESOLVE PROBLEMS?

CHAPTER ELEVEN

MORE ON QUESTIONS – DESIGNING, PURPOSE, SCENARIO AND USE

- **DON'T ASSUME ANYTHING WHEN NEGOTIATING – ASK IF YOU ARE NOT SURE OR YOU NEED TO VERIFY OR CLARIFY OPPONENT'S VIEWPOINT**
- **REFRAIN FROM QUESTIONS WITH "YES" OR "NO" ANSWERS**
- **CHECK UNDERSTANDING/LEVEL OF INTEREST – AVOID CONFUSION**
- **DETERMINE BEHAVIOR STYLE**
  - WHAT TYPE OF PERSON IS YOUR OPPONENT?

  - IS HE/SHE AN EXPERIENCED NEGOTIATOR? HOW DO YOU KNOW?

  - DECISIVE?

  - THOROUGH?

- **GAIN PARTICIPATION**
  - WHEN YOU ASK QUESTIONS, YOU GAIN IN EIGHT AREAS:

    - YOUR OPPONENT LIKES YOU BETTER, WHICH SIMPLY MEANS NEGOTIATIONS WILL GO BETTER

- YOU WILL LEARN MORE ABOUT YOUR OPPONENT THAN HE WILL LEARN ABOUT YOU

- ASKING QUESTIONS TELLS YOUR OPPONENT THAT YOU ARE INTERESTED IN THEM AND WHAT THEY HAVE TO SAY

- YOUR OPPONENT MAY HAVE TROUBLE GETTING TO THE POINT – QUESTIONS HELP BRING ATTENTION BACK TO THE SUBJECT

- QUESTIONS TEST YOUR OPPONENT'S TRUE ASPIRATIONS AND READINESS

- NEGOTIATIONS CAN BECOME TENSE. ASKING QUESTIONS ABOUT YOUR OPPONENT'S VIEWPOINT CAN BE HELPFUL

- QUESTIONS CAN INTRODUCE HUMOR TO REDUCE TENSION

- QUESTIONS CAN BE USED TO GIVE POSITIVE STROKES

- **LET'S LOOK AT MORE ON QUESTIONING TECHNIQUES WITH EMPHASIS ON:**
    - WHEN WORKING WITH A BUYER, A DIRECT QUESTION LIKE, "DO YOU HAVE THE GO-AHEAD FROM MANAGEMENT TO PURCHASE THIS TOOL BEFORE CLOSURE OF THE FISCAL YEAR?" ANOTHER TYPICAL QUESTION WOULD BE, "WHO ELSE NEEDS TO BE INVOLVED IN MAKING THIS TYPE

OF PURCHASE DECISION?" BASICALLY, YOU MUST DETERMINE WHAT INFORMATION WILL HELP YOU MAKE A GOOD DECISION, IF YOU WILL DISGUISE YOUR QUESTIONS, ETC.

- KNOW YOUR OPPONENT. IF YOU ARE RELATIONSHIP-ORIENTED AND YOU OPPONENT IS TASK-ORIENTED, YOUR EFFORTS TO INITIATE A LITTLE "SMALL TALK" MAY BE SEEN AS WASTING PRECIOUS TIME.

- WHAT MOTIVATES YOUR OPPONENT? WHAT ARE HIS/HER NEEDS AND VALUES? HIS/HER APPROACH TOWARD SOCIAL INTERACTIONS? A GREATER KNOWLEDGE OF THESE ISSUES WILL ENABLE YOU TO MAKE YOUR QUESTIONS MORE TARGETED AND SPECIFIC, AND THEREFORE MORE BENEFICIAL.

- MOVE FROM THE BROAD TO THE NARROW. START WITH BROAD QUESTIONS. THEN, AS YOU GAIN ANSWERS TO THESE, REFINE AND HONE YOUR QUESTIONS TO YIELD SPECIFIC INFORMATION. "HOW OFTEN DO YOU CHANGE YOUR OIL?" "EVERY THREE THOUSAND MILES" IS THE REPLY.

- USE GOOD TIMING AT THE NEGOTIATING TABLE. IF YOUR OPPONENT FINDS YOUR QUESTIONS OFFENSIVE, OR IF YOU INTERRUPT WHEN HE/SHE RESPONDS TO YOUR QUESTION(S), YOU MAY NOT GAIN THE INFORMATION YOU NEED, AND YOUR OPPONENT MAY BECOME RELUCTANT TO MEET WITH YOU IN THE FUTURE. STOP TALKING AFTER YOU ASK A QUESTION!!!

PURPOSEFUL QUESTIONS - SCENARIO

- **YOU ARE INTERVIEWING FOR A NEW SALES JOB. YOUR TWO MAIN GOALS ARE (1) SEEK MORE FLEXIBLE HOURS, AND (2) BE ABLE TO TELECOMMUNICATE A COUPLE DAYS EACH WEEK. LETS LOOK IN AT THE INTERVIEW NOW IN SESSION, AS YOU ASK QUESTIONS OF THE INTERVIEWER:**

  - GAIN INFORMATION: "WHAT SPECIFIC TYPES OF EXPERIENCE ARE YOU SEEKING IN THE SALES PERSON?"

  - CLARIFY OR VERIFY: "WHEN WOULD YOU WANT YOUR NEW EMPLOYEE TO START?"

  - CHECK UNDERSTANDING AND LEVEL OF INTEREST: "WHAT IS MORE IMPORTANT TO YOU – THAT THE SALESPERSON BE IN THE OFFICE 40 HOURS PER WEEK, OR THAT YOU INCREASE SALES THROUGH OTHER LEGAL MEANS?"

  - DETERMINE BEHAVIORAL STYLE: "WOULD YOU LIKE ME TO ROLE-PLAY A TYPICAL SALES SITUATION, OR WOULD YOU PREFER TO SEE STATISTICS THAT SHOW HOW MUCH I INCREASED SALES FOR MY PRESENT COMPANY?"

  - GIVE INFORMATION: "DID YOU KNOW THAT I AM FULLY SET UP TO WORK FROM MY HOME OFFICE AND, IN MY CURRENT POSITION, WORK TWO DAYS A WEEK FROM HOME?"

- START SOMEONE THINKING: "WHAT ATTRIBUTES DO YOU THINK ARE MOST IMPORTANT IN A SALESPERSON?"

- BRING ATTENTION BACK TO THE SUBJECT: "CAN YOU TALK MORE ABOUT FLEX TIME? ARE YOUR SALESPEOPLE IN THE OFFICE FROM 9:00 TO 5:00?"

- REACH AGREEMENT: "IF I COULD GUARANTEE AN INCREASE IN YOUR SALES VOLUME, WOULD YOU BE WILLING TO CONSIDER MORE FLEXIBLE WORK HOURS?"

- INCREASE RECEPTION TO YOUR IDEAS: "SINCE WE ARE ON THE WEST COAST, DO YOU THINK IT BEST TO CALL ON POTENTIAL CUSTOMERS ON THE EAST COAST IN THE MORNING?"

- REDUCE TENSION: WHENEVER I BRING UP THE SUBJECT OF FLEX TIME, YOU SEEM A LITTLE UNCOMFORTABLE. CAN YOU TELL ME WHY?"

- GIVE POSITIVE STROKES OR BUILD RAPPORT: "IT'S PRETTY FRUSTRATING WHEN YOU KNOW YOUR PRODUCT IS BETTER THAN ALL THE OTHERS ON THE MARKET, AND YET YOUR SALES ARE NOT WHAT THEY SHOULD BE ISN'T IT?"

CHAPTER TWELVE

WHAT DO YOU KNOW ABOUT NEGOTIATING? (ANSWER YES OR NO)

- **EMOTIONAL DISPLAYS DURING NEGOTIATING SESSIONS ARE OK**
  YES   NO*

- **SOMETIMES, YOU WILL NEED TO WALK AWAY FROM A NEGOTIATING SESSION**
  YES*   NO

- **"WIN-WIN" IS ALWAYS THE OBJECT OF BUSINESS NEGOTIATIONS**
  YES   NO*

- **WE ALL NEED VARIOUS THINGS; THEREFORE, IT IS OK TO DISPLAY YOUR NEED(S) WHILE NEGOTIATING**
  YES   NO*

- **SOME NEGOTIATORS ARE ACTUALLY CONSIDERED "TIGERS" AT THE NEGOTIATING TABLE BECAUSE OF SHEER AGGRESSIVENESS**
  YES*   NO

- **WE ANTICIPATE THAT ALL NEGOTIATORS MAY LOSE CONTROL FREQUENTLY**
  YES   NO*

- **A HIGH-PITCHED VOICE AND RUSHED VOICE COULD BE SIGNS OF NEED, OR EVEN FRUSTRATION**
  YES*   NO

- **YOU <u>CANNOT</u> BE REJECTED AT THE NEGOTIATING TABLE**
  YES   NO*

- **THE WORDS, "THIS IS MY FINAL OFFER" CONSTITUTE THE MOST COMMON BLUFF**
  YES*   NO

- **CAR DEALERS ARE RESPECTED BECAUSE OF THEIR TOUGH JOB**
  YES   NO*

- **BUYERS CAN EXPERIENCE REMORSE**
  YES*   NO

- **AN EXAMPLE OF BUYER REMORSE IS (CIRCLE ONE)**
  "HOW WILL I PAY FOR THIS CAR?" – YES*

  "MY OPPONENT LOST HIS SHIRT!" - NO

- **FROM A NEGOTIATING POINT OF VIEW, PURCHASING A CAR IS NO DIFFERENT THAN BUYING A SUIT**
  YES*   NO

- **YOU HEARD IN A DISCUSSION BETWEEN TWO CAR SALESPERSONS:**

"RELAX. THE LONGER THEY NEGOTIATE, THE HARDER IT IS FOR THEM TO WALK AWAY"
YES*   NO

- ### YOUR ADVERSARY DOES NOT WANT TO BE YOUR FRIEND. DO YOU AGREE?
  YES*   NO

- ### RESEARCH IS ESSENTIAL TO A SUCCESSFUL NEGOTIATING SESSION. AGREE?
  YES*   NO

- ### NAME THREE SOURCES OF INFORMATION WHEN CONDUCTING MEANINGFUL RESEARCH
  1. D+B
  2. B+B
  3. COMPETITION

- ### (1) AN AGENDA HELPS BUILD EMOTIONAL CONTROL, BUT (2) IS ALWAYS CRITICAL TO THE NEGOTIATING PROCESS
  (1) YES   (2) NO*   (3) UNDECIDED

- ### BRIEFLY STATE THE DIFFERENCE BETWEEN OPEN-ENDED AND CLOSED-ENDED QUESTIONS. GIVE AT LEAST ONE EXAMPLE.

- ### THE PERSON SPEAKING ALWAYS HAS CONTROL OVER THE SESSION
  YES*   NO

- **GIVE ONE EXAMPLE OF NON-VERBAL EXPRESSION IN NEGOTIATING**
    1. FACIAL VIEW

- **PARAPHRASING IS OK WHEN VISITING YOUR DOCTOR, BUT NOT IN NEGOTIATING**
    YES   NO*

- **WHEN IT COMES TO NEGOTIATING, THERE IS A DEFINITE GENDER DIFFERENCE**
    YES*   NO

- **THE CONSEQUENCES OF DEADLOCK ARE USUALLY WORSE FOR THE SELLER**
    YES*   NO

- **<u>WORST WORDS</u> FOR THE SELLER ARE – "I'LL NEED MORE TIME TO THINK ABOUT IT"**
    YES*   NO

- **BUYERS CAN "NIBBLE" AT SELLER'S SOFT UNDERBELLY**
    YES*   NO

- **AMATEURS OFTEN FAIL TO SEE OPTIONS**
    YES*   NO   N/A

- **HE WHO DEFINES THE ISSUES AND DETERMINES THEIR PRIORITY IS ALREADY WELL ON THE WAY TO WINNING**
    YES*   NO

- **THE BEST NEGOTIATORS ARE THOSE THAT REGULARLY ASK OPEN-ENDED QUESTIONS**
  YES*   NO

- **ONCE YOU DECIDE NOT TO REWARD INTIMIDATION, YOU HAVE A WHOLE NEW BALL GAME**
  YES*   NO   ADVERSARIAL DECISION   N/A

- **NEGOTIATING SHOULD BE A PROCESS OF RECIPROCITY IF IT IS TO WORK WELL**
  YES*   NO   N/A

- **WHICH OF THE FOLLOWING ITEMS (2) MIGHT COME FROM A POWER NEGOTIATOR?**
  - *TAKE THOSE PHONE CALLS DURING THE NEGOTIATING SESSION. AFTER ALL, YOU ARE A BUSY MAN

  - *INTIMIDATE YOUR OPPONENT WITH THE TRAPPINGS OF POWER (WINDOW, BIG DESK, PLAQUES, ETC)

  - ENGAGE IN SMALL TALK BEFORE THE NEGOTIATING SESSION BEGINS

- **APPROXIMATELY WHAT PERCENT OF WOMEN WOULD RATHER HAVE A ROOT CANAL (WITH A POSTHOLE DIGGER) THAN NEGOTIATE THE SALE OF A NEW CAR?**
  7%   49%   93%*   100%   NONE

CHAPTER THIRTEEN

NEGOTIATING FOR REAL – A CASE STUDY

- <u>SETTING</u>: PETER OWNS AC ENTERPRISES. HE GIVES ADVICE AND TRAINING IN INSTALLING NEW SYSTEMS, ESPECIALLY COMPUTER SYSTEMS. TODAY'S NEGOTIATION IS WITH HENRY, A SENIOR MANAGER WITH WESTERN CORPORATION. PETER KNOWS THAT HENRY IS A TOUGH NEGOTIATOR. HENRY LIKES TO START WITH A LITTLE WARM-UP PERIOD. PETER PREVIOUSLY COMPLETED SEVERAL PROJECTS FOR HENRY. THE PROJECT BEING NEGOTIATED TODAY IS VALUED AT $220,000. AFTER A BRIEF WAIT, PETER IS INVITED INTO HENRY'S OFFICE. AS HE ENTERS, HENRY WALKS TOWARD HIM, SMILES AND SHAKES HIS HAND. "THANKS FOR COMING, PETER. HOW ARE YOU TODAY?"

- "FINE, HENRY. DID YOU GET A CHANCE TO READ MY PROPOSAL?"

- HENRY FROWNS SLIGHTLY AT PETER'S ABRUPTNESS, THEN SAYS: "YES, AND IT SEEMS TO SATISFY MOST OF OUR NEEDS."

- PETER MISSES THE SIGNIFICANCE OF THE WORD "MOST" AND CONTINUES,

- "I'M SURE YOU WILL FIND IT IS AN EXCELLENT PROPOSAL."

- **PETER, I HAVE A LOT OF CONFIDENCE IN YOUR FIRM. YOU HAVE ALWAYS DONE EXCELLENT WORK FOR US."**

- "THANK YOU, HENRY."

- **"BUT I AM CONCERNED ABOUT THE TRAINING," SAID HENRY.**

- **PETER IS A BIT SURPRISED.**

- "OH?"

- **"YOU SAID THAT ONE OF YOUR PEOPLE WILL DO IT."**

- "THAT IS CORRECT."

- **"WELL, WE HAVE A QUALIFIED PERSON WHO COULD DO IT. HER NAME IS BETTY MCINTYRE. HERE IS HER RESUME." HENRY HANDS PETER THE RESUME AND SITS BACK, WAITING FOR HIM TO READ IT."**

- **PETER DOES NOT EVEN LOOK AT IT BECAUSE HE HAS ALREADY DISMISSED THE IDEA OF USING BETTY.**

- "WELL, HENRY, WE'VE FOUND THAT OUR STAFF DOES A MUCH BETTER JOB THAN INTERNAL PEOPLE."

- **HENRY STARTS TO OBJECT, "PERHAPS, BUT . . ."**

- PETER INTERRUPTS. "USING ONE OF OUR TRAINED CONSULTANTS WOULD PROVIDE MUCH BETTER QUALITY CONTROL."

- **HENRY IS OBVIOUSLY ANNOYED. "BEFORE YOU JUMP TO CONCLUSIONS, LET ME TELL YOU A LITTLE ABOUT BETTY. SHE IS FAIRLY NEW TO MY COMPANY, BUT SHE HAS AN EXCELLENT BACKGROUND IN COMPUTER SYSTEMS. SHE ALSO HAS CONDUCTED NUMEROUS TRAINING SEMINARS."**

- **PETER IGNORES HENRY'S POINT AND BLUNDERS ON.**

- "I DON'T DOUBT HER QUALIFICATIONS, HENRY, BUT THE ONLY WAY WE CAN GUARANTEE THE RESULTS YOU WANT IS TO DO THE TRAINING OURSELVES."

- **HENRY, BECOMING MORE ANNOYED, FLATLY STATES," I WANT BETTY TO DO IT."**

- "BE REASONABLE, HENRY. YOUR EQUIPMENT ARRIVES IN SIX WEEKS. IF WE HAD TO TRAIN BETTY, AND THEN WAIT FOR HER TO TRAIN YOUR PEOPLE, WE'D NEVER FINISH ON TIME."

- **"IF NECESSARY, WE COULD DELAY ARRIVAL OF THE EQUIPMENT," SAID HENRY.**

- **PETER IS ASTONISHED.**

- "WHAT? I THOUGHT THE SCHEDULE WAS YOUR KEY PROJECT."

- **"NO, IT IS IMPORTANT, BUT NOT AS IMPORTANT AS HAVING BETTY ON THE PROJECT."**

- **PETER IS NOW QUITE EXASPERATED.**

- "HENRY, THIS JUST DOES NOT MAKE SENSE. WHY DELAY SUCH AN IMPORTANT PROJECT WHEN WE ARE TOTALLY QUALIFIED TO DO THE TRAINING WITHIN THE ORIGINAL SCHEDULE?"

- **"THERE ARE A COUPLE OF IMPORTANT REASONS. FIRST, I WANT TO DEVELOP HER FOR SOME OTHER THINGS, AND SHE NEEDS THIS VISIBILITY. SECOND, IT WILL SAVE US SOME MONEY."**

- **PETER IGNORES THE SECOND POINT AND SAYS,**

- "OH, YOU WOULD NOT SAVE THAT MUCH."

- **"HOW MUCH?", ASKS HENRY.**

- **SINCE HE IS UNPREPARED FOR THE QUESTION, PETER STALLS, JOTS DOWN SOME QUESTIONS, THEN REPLIES,**

- "WELL, LET'S SEE . . . OUR ORIGINAL PROPOSAL WAS FOR $220,000 . . . ABOUT $10,000 OF THAT WAS FOR TRAINING."

- **"SO, WE COULD SAVE $10,000 IF SHE DID THE TRAINING?"**

- "NO . . . WE WOULD STILL HAVE TO TRAIN AND SUPERVISE BETTY."

- **"SO, HOW MUCH WOULD THAT COST?"**

- "I COULDN'T SAY," SAID PETER. "WE HAVE NOT EVEN CONSIDERED THE POSSIBILITY."

- **FROWNING, HENRY SAYS, "I SEE."**

- "HENRY, THIS JUST DOES NOT MAKE SENSE. THE MONEY TO SAVE ON OUR FEE WOULD BE LESS THAN WHAT YOU WOULD SPEND ON BETTY'S TIME."

- **"PETER," HENRY PAUSES FOR EMPHASIS AND SPEAKS VERY FIRMLY, "BETTY CANNOT BE CUT OUT OF THIS PROCESS. IT'S JUST AS SIMPLE AS THAT."**

- **BY NOW, PETER IS SO FRUSTRATED THAT HE DOES NOT KNOW WHAT TO DO.**

- "HENRY, COULD WE JUST SET THIS WHOLE ISSUE OF TRAINING ASIDE AND TALK ABOUT THE PRICE AND EVERYTHING ELSE?"

- **HENRY ABRUPTLY PUSHES BACK FROM HIS DESK AND SAYS, "I'M NOT READY TO TALK PRICE YET. YOU FIGURE OUT HOW MUCH YOU CAN REDUCE YOUR BID BY USING BETTY, AND THEN GET**

BACK TO ME." HE THEN STANDS UP AND WALKS AROUND THE DESK, DISMISSING PETER.

- PETER LOOKS STUNNED AS HE RISES FROM HIS CHAIR AND SHAKES HENRY'S HAND.

- "OKAY . . . I WILL PUT SOME NUMBERS TOGETHER AND GET BACK TO YOU TOMORROW. HOW DOES THAT SOUND?"

- **"FINE, THANKS FOR YOUR TIME."**

- PETER LEAVES.

OK . . . IT'S TIME TO ANALYZE THIS MATTER.

- WAS HENRY CORRECT IN INSISTING ON USE OF AN IN-HOUSE STAFF MEMBER TO CONDUCT TRAINING?

- IS PETER RUNNING THE RISK OF LOSING THE CONTRACT? COULD HE LOSE ALL FUTURE BUSINESS WITH HENRY

- WHAT WOULD YOU DO IF YOU WERE HENRY? HOW ABOUT PETER?

- HOW WOULD YOU ADDRESS THIS MATTER?

- WHO IS THE "BAD GUY" HERE?

CHAPTER FOURTEEN

ON INTIMIDATION

- **IF OPPONENT USES HARDBALL TACTICS, YOUR BEST REACTION IS NO REACTION AT ALL!!**
    - YOU WILL APPEAR CONFIDENT AND IN CONTROL

    - IRONY – THEY WILL END UP BEING THE PARTY THAT IS INTIMIDATED, NOT YOU!!

    - ONCE YOU DECIDE NOT TO REWARD INTIMIDATION, YOU WILL HAVE A WHOLE NEW BALL GAME.

- **A COMMON TACTIC USED BY HARDBALL NEGOTIATORS IS TO ARGUE ABOUT ANY POSITION YOU TAKE WITHOUT OFFERING A COUNTER-OFFER**
    - NEGOTIATING MUST BE A PROCESS OF RECIPROCITY IF IT IS TO WORK

    - ONCE YOU MAKE AN OFFER WHICH OPPONENT REFUSES TO ACCEPT, ASK FOR A COUNTER-OFFER

CHAPTER FIFTEEN

POWER NEGOTIATING – WINNING AT ALL COSTS!!

- **MAKE THEM MEET YOU ON YOUR TURF – YOUR OFFICE OR A LOCATION SELECTED BY YOU**
  - YOU HAVE THE PSYCHOLOGICAL ADVANTAGE WHEN YOU NAME THE MEETING LOCATION
- **LET THEM WAIT – YOU ARE A BUSY PERSON!**
- **INTIMIDATE THEM WITH THE TRAPPINGS OF POWER AT YOUR OFFICE – BIG BUILDING, LARGE CHAIR, WINDOWS, SECRETARY, AND OVERALL IMPRESSIVE SURROUNDINGS!!**
- **SHOW OFF YOUR ACCOMPLISHMENTS – PLAQUES, CERTIFICATES, ETC.**
- **PUT THEM IN FRONT OF YOUR BIG, IMPRESSIVE DESK. MAKE THEM SIT IN A HARD-BACK CHAIR – YOU IN AN IMPRESSIVE PADDED CHAIR**
- **SMOKE IF YOU LIKE. IF THE SMOKE IMPACTS THEM, ALL THE BETTER. AFTER ALL, THIS IS <u>YOUR</u> OFFICE!!**
- **TAKE THOSE CALLS IF YOU LIKE. AFTER ALL, YOU ARE A BUSY PERSON!!**
- **DRIVE THEIR OFFER DOWN RIGHT AWAY!! SHOW THEM YOU WON'T BE FOOLED BY A STACK OF SPREAD SHEETS, COST ESTIMATES, ETC. WHAT CAN IT HURT?**
- **ACT LIKE YOU ARE DOING THEM A FAVOR JUST TO HAVE THEM COME TO YOUR OFFICE AND LISTENING TO THEIR PITCH**

- **CONTROL OR INFLUENCE THE GROUND RULES OF THE AGENDA**
- **LET YOUR OPPONENT KNOW THAT YOU DON'T SURRENDER, YOU DON'T CONCEDE, AND YOU DON'T GIVE UP ANYTHING WITHOUT GETTING SOMETHING OF EQUAL OR GREATER VALUE IN RETURN**
- **ALSO, LET YOUR OPPONENT KNOW THAT YOU RARELY BEND AND GENERALLY EXHIBIT ALL THE MOBILITY, FLEXIBILITY, GENEROSITY AND OPENNESS OF A PARK STATUE**
  - NOTE 1: POWER NEGOTIATORS ARE OFTEN AGGRESSIVE, DOMINEERING, AND EVEN BELLIGERENT. HE OR SHE IS DEMANDING AND PUSHY, DISGUISING AIMS UNDER A CONTRIVED PLEASANT DEMEANOR. THE OBJECTIVE IS CLEAR – WIN AT ALL COST!!

  - NOTE 2: IS IT POSSIBLE TO EFFECTIVELY NEGOTIATE DEALS THAT BRING VALUE TO ALL PARTIES, TO DISPLAY EMPATHY AND FAIRNESS?

  - NOTE 3: CAN YOU NAME FIVE OTHER WAYS TO DEMONSTRATE YOU ARE A POWER NEGOTIATOR?

CHAPTER SIXTEEN

NEGOTIATING WITH DIFFICULT PEOPLE

- **FIVE TYPICAL CATEGORIES**
    - BULLIES – THEY VERBALLY OR EVEN PHYSICALLY ATTACK, USE THREATS, DEMANDS OR ATTEMPT TO INTIMIDATE. THEY SAY THINGS LIKE, "THAT IS A STUPID THING YOU SAID."

    - AVOIDERS – THEY PHYSICALLY AVOID OR PROCRASTINATE, HIDE OR REFUSE TO NEGOTIATE. TYPICAL STATEMENT: "THAT IS NOT MY PROBLEM"

    - WITHDRAWERS – THEY EMOTIONALLY WITHDRAW, GET CONFUSED, GO DUMB. YOU'LL HEAR THEM SAY, "I DON'T UNDERSTAND!!"

    - HIGH ROLLERS – THEY ATTEMPT TO SHOCK AND INTIMIDATE THEIR OPPOSITION BY MAKING EXTREME DEMANDS LIKE, "I WANT IT ALL DONE BY NOON OR ELSE!"

    - WAD SHOOTERS – THEY ASSUME AN ALL-OR-NOTHING, TAKE-IT-OR-LEAVE-IT STANCE. "IF YOU DON'T WANT IT, FORGET IT!"

- **TYPICAL RESPONSE TO DIFFICULT PEOPLE**
  - <u>GET THEIR ATTENTION</u> – DRAW A BOUNDARY AND MEAN IT. STATE YOUR POSITION AND DON'T BACK DOWN

  - <u>CALL A SPADE A SPADE</u> – IDENTIFY THE PROBLEM BEHAVIOR AND INVITE HIM/HER TO BE MORE CONSTRUCTIVE. EXPLAINING THAT HE/SHE IS BEING A BULLY HELPS THE PERSON BECOME CONSCIOUS OF BEHAVIOR. STATEMENT: "YOUR REPEATED ATTACKS ARE NOT GETTING US ANY CLOSER TO AN AGREEMENT"

- **PUTTING THEIR FEARS TO REST – ESPECIALLY WHEN DEALING WITH AVOIDERS OR WITHDRAWERS**
  - <u>DON'T BE DEFENSIVE</u> – "WOULD YOU FEEL MORE COMFORTABLE IF WE MEET IN YOUR OFFICE?"

  - <u>RESPOND TO NEEDS</u> – "I CAN SEE HOW YOU FEEL FRUSTRATED."

  - <u>ACTIVELY LISTEN</u> – "WHAT I HEAR YOU SAYING IS ....."

  - <u>DON'T COUNTERATTACK</u> – HELPING BULLIES FEEL SAFER MAY SEEM COUNTERINTUITIVE, BUT THAT IS EXACTLY WHAT YOU NEED TO DO

- **INSIST ON PLAYING BY THE RULES – BULLIES, HIGH ROLLERS AND WAD SHOOTERS WILL ATTEMPT TO FORCE YOU TO ACCEPT UNREASONABLE DEMANDS. "I REFUSE TO BE PRESSURED INTO AN AGREEMENT"**

- **REFUSE TO BE PUNISHED – NO ONE HAS THE RIGHT TO PUNISH YOU. DRAW A BOUNDARY BY ASKING THE OTHER PERSON WHAT THEY WANT. IF THE RESPONSE IS, "I DON'T KNOW," INFORM HIM/HER THAT YOU ARE NOT WILLING TO CONTINUE THE DISCUSSION WHEN THEY DO NOT KNOW, AND THAT YOU ARE NOT WILLING TO BE PUNISHED.**
- **ASK QUESTIONS – ASKING QUESTIONS INVITES THE OTHER PERSON TO JUSTIFY THEIR POSITION OR VENT THEIR FEELINGS. "WHAT" QUESTIONS WILL KEEP THE QUESTIONS MOVING. "WHY" QUESTIONS WILL TEND TO LEAD YOU TO BATTLE POSITIONS. "WHY DID YOU DO THAT?"**
- **POINT OUT THE CONSEQUENCES – "THE REALITY IS, IF WE LOSE ANOTHER MILLION DOLLARS NEXT MONTH, WE WILL BE FORCED TO LAY OFF 50 PEOPLE." PRESENT YOUR ARGUMENT AS A STATEMENT OF INEVITABLE CONSEQUENCES RATHER THAN A THREAT.**

CHAPTER SEVENTEEN

PULLING TEETH, OR MAKING THEM SAY "UNCLE"

- **THE SAVVY CONSULTANT WILL TELL YOU TO APPROACH NEGOTIATING WITH A WIN-WIN PHILOSOPHY. THEN HE/SHE OFFERS THESE TRICKS:**
    - GET YOUR OPPONENT TO TRAVEL TO YOUR CITY

    - CALL EARLY MORNING MEETING SO THEY ARE SUFFERING FROM JET LAG, AND NOT OPERATING AT PEAK MENTAL EFFICIENCY

    - DURING THE MEETING, FOCUS ON DISCOVERING THE OTHER PERSON'S WEAKNESSES. WHAT NEED OR WEAKNESS DOES THE PERSON HAVE THAT YOU CAN EXPLOIT?

- **IF THE OTHER PERSON WON'T LOOK YOU IN THE EYE WHEN HE/SHE SPEAKS, OR KICKS HIS/HER FEET OR RUBS HIS NECK, HE/SHE PROBABLY IS NOT TELLING THE TRUTH, PER THE CONSULTANT.**
- **THE CONSULTANT ALSO OFFERS PRINCIPLES OF NEGOTIATING:**
    - MAKE YOUR NEGOTIATING OPPONENT FULLY AWARE OF YOUR POWER

- TRY TO DISCOVER EARLY YOUR OPPONENT'S MOTIVE OR EVERY NEGOTIATING POSITION/ACTION

- CONTROL OR INFLUENCE THE GROUND RULES AND THE AGENDA

- **IS THIS YOUR STYLE? HOW DO YOU KNOW? DOES IT FIT YOU? DO YOU AGREE WITH THE CONSULTANT? IS THIS CONSIDERED "WIN-WIN" OR "WIN-LOST" NEGOTIATING, OR SOMEWHERE BETWEEN? COULD YOU CONSIDER THIS "POWER NEGOTIATION?" THE POWER NEGOTIATOR WANTS TO DEFEAT THE OTHER PARTY, USUALLY AT ALL COSTS. WINNING BECOMES MORE IMPORTANT THAN THE DEAL ITSELF.**

CHAPTER EIGHTEEN

DIRTY TRICKS, NASTY GIMMICKS/ TERMS (BOTH PRE/PAST)

- **THE AFTERBITE**
  - DEMANDING SOMETHING EXTRA AFTER YOU'VE ALREADY COMPLETED THE DEAL

- **BLANKETING**
  - LOADING UP THE NEGOTIATING SESSION WITH TONS OF PAPER, SPREADSHEETS, DOZENS OF TEAM MEMBERS SO YOU FEEL INTIMIDATED BY THE SHEER NUMBERS

- **BRACKETING**
  - "HOW MUCH DO YOU WANT TO PAY PER MONTH?" WHEN BUYING A CAR – RATHER THAN DEAL OVER THE COST OF THE AUTO

- **DEADLINES**
  - "ANOTHER PERSON IS LOOKING AT THIS CAR, AND HE PLAN S TO RETURN TOMORROW." TIME PUTS PRESSURE ON YOU FOR A QUICK DECISION

- **DELAYING**
  - OFTEN USED TO BUY TIME TO NEGOTIATE WITH ONE OF YOUR COMPETITORS

- **FALSE INFORMATION**
  - OUTRIGHT LYING

- **THE FEINT**
  - DIVERTING YOUR ATTENTION FROM THE TOPIC THEY THINK IS CRUCIAL

- **FINE PRINT**
  - ADDING PROVISIONS THAT WERE NOT PART OF THE ORIGINAL DEAL

- **FUNNY MONEY**
  - HIDDEN COSTS THAT WERE NEVER MENTIONED UNTIL AFTER THE DEAL IS COMPLETE – SUCH AS TAXES, SHIPPING, DOCK FEES, COPYING, HANDLING, DOCUMENT FEES, OTHER

- **GOOD GUY/BAD GUY**
  - A CLASSIC – PITTING THE SEEMINGLY HOSTILE NEGOTIATOR AGAINST YOU WHILE THE NICER PARTNER INTERVENES

- **INTIMIDATION**
  - EMPLOYING LARGE, LOUD, AGGRESSIVE OR BULLYING NEGOTIATORS, SMOKE-FILLED MEETING ROOMS, MALE CONDESCENSION TOWARD FEMALES

- **LIMITED AUTHORITY**
  - "I CANNOT CLOSE THE DEAL WITHOUT FIRST DISCUSSING WITH MY BOSS." THIS PLACES BLAME FOR AGGRESSIVE TACTICS ON SOME THIRD PARTY AND ALLOWS SPOKESPERSON TO PRETEND TO BE RESPONSIBLE TO DIRECTION FROM ELSEWHERE

- **SALAMI**
  - NEGOTIATING PIECE-BY-PIECE RATHER THAN FROM THE BIG PICTURE. CAN BE RATHER EXPENSIVE

- **SURPRISE**
  - SUDDEN POSITION SHIFT TO THROW YOU OFF

- **TAKE IT OR LEAVE IT**
  - THE BEST WAY TO RESPOND TO THESE TRICKS/ TRAPS IS TO RECOGNIZE THEM FOR WHAT THEY ARE AND THEN GRACEFULLY SIDE STEP THEM. THIS IS THE MOST FREQUENTLY USED "BULLY" TACTIC IN THE NEGOTIATING ARENA

CHAPTER NINETEEN

THE TESTOSTERONE FACTOR: DO MEN AND WOMEN NEGOTIATE DIFFERENTLY?

- **QUESTION: IN YOUR VIEW, ARE MEN AND WOMEN DIFFERENT WHEN IT COMES TO NEGOTIATING?**
- **YES ___**
- **NO ___**
- **WOMEN ARE:**
  - LESS LIKELY THAN MEN TO ENROLL IN COMPANY TRAINING PROGRAMS ON THE SUBJECT

  - MAKE UP A SMALLER FRACTION OF READERS OF BOOKS ON NEGOTIATING

  - LESS INCLINED TO ATTEND PUBLIC SEMINARS ON NEGOTIATING THAN DO MEN

- **EXIT POLLS OF WOMEN WHO DO ATTEND NEGOTIATING SEMINARS FIND THE IDEA OF HAVING TO NEGOTIATE VERY DISTASTEFUL**
  - BECAUSE NEGOTIATING IS AN INESCAPABLE ASPECT OF OUR LIVES, KEY RESEARCHERS BELIEVE THAT WOMEN ARE AT A DISADVANTAGE IN SUCH SITUATIONS

  - KEY FEMINIST BUSINESS WRITERS HAVE COMMENTED ON THE APPARENT DIFFERENCES IN ATTITUDES THAT MEN AND WOMEN BRING TO THE NEGOTIATING TABLE

- BECAUSE FEW CHIEF EXECUTIVES ARE FEMALE, THE ASSUMPTIONS AND HABITS THAT DOMINATE THE NEGOTIATING WORLD TEND TO BE THOSE OF MEN

- **MANY MEN SUBSCRIBE, CONSCIOUSLY OR UNCONSCIOUSLY, TO SO-CALLED "WARRIOR" VALUES IN BUSINESS AND NEGOTIATING. THE FIGURES OF SPEECH THEY USE TO DESCRIBE BUSINESS DEALS ARE OFTEN THE METAPHORS OF WARFARE, COMBAT, TACTICS AND SPORTS. WOMEN GENERALLY FIND THIS DISTASTEFUL AND ARE NOT FULLY COMFORTABLE WITH THE FRAME OF REFERENCE OF WARFARE IN NEGOTIATING**

  - MEN ASSIGN LOWER PRIORITIES TO SOCIAL ISSUES, EMPATHY, AVOIDANCE OF CONFLICT AND HUMAN NEEDS THAN THEY ASSIGN TO ACHIEVING GOALS AND GETTING WORK DONE

  - WHETHER THESE DIFFERENCES ARE BIOLOGICALLY OR CULTURALLY ACQUIRED, OR BOTH, IS LESS IMPORTANT THAN RECONCILING THEM SO BOTH MEN AND WOMEN CAN FEEL COMFORTABLE AND BE EFFECTIVE IN NEGOTIATING AND OBTAINING GOOD DEALS FOR THEMSELVES OR THE CORPORATION

- **THIS MATERIAL IS NEITHER MALE NOR FEMALE IN ITS DESIGN. IT TENDS TO BE SOMEWHAT ANDROGYNOUS, APPEALING TO THE NEEDS OF BOTH GENDERS. IT IS AN APPROACH WHICH EMPHASIZES MAXIMIZATION OF VALUE, NOT JUST THE CONCEPT OF DEFEATING PEOPLE.**

CHAPTER TWENTY

CONTROL MOMENTUM

- **THE BUYER AND SUPPLIER MET AGAIN THIS MORNING, IN AN ATTEMPT TO CLOSEOUT THE DEAL. THEY BOTH AGREED BETTY WOULD DO THE TRAINING. THIS SOLVED THE TRAINING ISSUE. WHEN THE MEETING RECONVENED, THE BUYER LEANED FORWARD AND SAID, "NOW, WITH THE TRAINING MATTER RESOLVED, WE WILL GET A BREAK ON THE PRICE, RIGHT?"**

- UNFORTUNATELY, PETER MISSED THE POINT. "LET'S SEE . . ." HE STARTS TO SAY SOMETHING.

- **THE BUYER SAID, "PETER, YOU SAID THE COST OF THE TRAINER WAS $10,000, SO WE CAN NOW SUBTRACT THAT AMOUNT. CORRECT?"**

- "NO," SAID PETER. "WE HAVE TO PUT IN THE COST OF TRAINING AND SUPERVISING BETTY, WHICH IN REALITY IS ABOUT $5,000."

- **"SO, YOUR BID IS NOW $5,000 LESS. CORRECT?"**

- "YES"

- **"COME ON. I'VE BEEN DOING A LITTLE CHECKING AND I FIGURE YOUR COSTS ARE SOMEWHERE BETWEEN $____ AND $____"**

- PETER LOOKS SURPRISED, BECAUSE THE ESTIMATE IS QUITE ACCURATE. "REALLY . . . ?"

- **THE BUYER JOTS DOWN A FEW FIGURES. HE SAYS, "A FAIR PROFIT WOULD BE 10%. LET'S SEE, ADD 10% AND WE WOULD BE WORKING WITH A FAIR PRICE FOR THE JOB."**

<u>NOTE</u>: PETER IS FLABBERGASTED. SINCE HE EXPECTED THE BUYER TO RESPOND POSITIVELY TO HIS FLEXIBILITY ON THE TRAINING ISSUE, HE DOES NOT KNOW HOW TO RESPOND TO THIS ATTACKING OFFER. PETER FORGOT THAT THE BUYER LOVES TO PLAY BARGAINING GAMES.

- PETER SAID, "THAT IS IMPOSSIBLE!!! . . . THERE IS NO WAY WE CAN DO THE JOB FOR THAT AMOUNT."
- "WELL, THERE IS A LITTLE ROOM, BUT NOT MUCH." PETER PAUSES, THEN CONTINUES, "IF BETTY IS AS GOOD AS YOU SAY, WE COULD PROBABLY SHORTEN OUR TIME FOR TRAINING AND SUPERVISING HER." AFTER USING HIS CALCULATOR, HE SAYS, "I GUESS I CAN REDUCE THE PRICE BY 3%."
- **"PETER, YOU ARE TRYING TO MAKE ABOUT $30,000 PROFIT ON THIS DEAL." SHAKING HIS HEAD, THE BUYER ADDS, "THAT IS TOO MUCH PROFIT FOR A CONTRACT LIKE THIS."**
- PETER SAID, "I'VE OFFERED YOU A VERY GOOD PRICE FOR THE QUALITY WE DELIVER."
- **THE BUYER REACHES FOR A PIECE OF PAPER, WRITES A NUMBER ON THE SHEET, FOLDS THE PAPER, AND HANDS IT TO PETER.**
- AFTER LOOKING AT THE PAPER, PETER SHAKES HIS HEAD AND CROSSES HIS ARMS. "THAT'S TOTALLY OUT OF THE QUESTION!!"
- **"WELL, SO IS YOUR NUMBER." THE BUYER INDIRECTLY ACKNOWLEDGES THAT HIS OFFER IS UNREASONABLE, BUT PETER DOES NOT PICK UP ON THE SIGNAL.**
- PETER JOTS DOWN SOME NUMBERS ON A SHEET, AND PASSES IT BACK TO THE BUYER.

- **"THAT IS A LITTLE BETTER, BUT IT IS STILL NOT A NUMBER I CAN LIVE WITH."**
- "I HAVE COME DOWN A LOT," SAID PETER
- **"I REALIZE THAT – AND I WILL RETURN THE FAVOR." HE WRITES A NUMBER ON THE PAPER, AND PASSES IT BACK TO PETER.**
- PETER SHAKES HIS HEAD AFTER READING THE NEW NUMBERS. HE RISES SLOWLY FROM HIS CHAIR AND WALKS OVER TO THE WINDOW. AFTER A FEW MOMENTS, HE TURNS TOWARD THE BUYER AND SAYS, "I CAN SHAVE AN ADDITIONAL $2,000, BUT THAT IS JUGGLING A LOT OF NUMBERS, AND IT ALSO REPRESENTS MY FINAL NUMBER. THE SENIOR PARTNER IN THE CORPORATION WILL HAVE MY HEAD."
- **"PETER, WE MUST REDUCE THE PRICE SOMEHOW, EXACTLY WHAT CAN YOU DO? I THINK I HAVE BEEN MORE THAN FAIR, AS I HAVE BEEN IN OTHER NEGOTIATING SESSIONS. I DON'T WANT TO JEOPARDIZE THIS DEAL. MY POCKETS AREN'T LINED WITH GOLD." AT THIS POINT, THE BUYER KNOWS HE HAS THE UPPER HAND, HE IS SATISFIED, SMILING INWARD, BUT IS TRYING FOR MORE.**
- "1,000 MORE. THAT IS ALL!!" PETER HAD NOW GIVEN TWO CONCESSIONS IN A ROW, WHICH IS A "NO-NO" FOR A BUYER OR A SELLER. DON'T DO IT!!
- **"OK, PETER. DROP YOUR PRICE BY ANOTHER $500, AND WE WILL CLOSE THIS DEAL."**
- PETER FURROWS HIS BROW, THINKS IT OVER, LOWERS HIS HEAD. THEN HE SAYS, "WELL, YOU'D BETTER INTRODUCE ME TO BETTY. LOOKS LIKE WE WILL BE WORKING TOGETHER!!"

CHAPTER TWENTY-ONE

BUSINESS RATIOS AND SOLVENCY

- SOLVENCY REFERS TO THE ABILITY OF A FIRM TO PAY ITS DEBTS AS THEY BECOME DUE. THE PRIMARY MEASURES OF SHORT-TERM SOLVENCY ARE THE CURRENT RATIO, QUICK RATIO, INVENTORY TURNOVER, NUMBER OF DAYS RECEIVABLES OUTSTANDING, DEBT TO EQUITY RATIO, TIMES INTEREST EARNED AND ASSET TURNOVER. OTHER BUSINESS RATIOS ARE USED LESS OFTEN, AND NOT ADDRESSED HEREIN. PROCUREMENT, ACCOUNTING AND OTHER BUSINESS PERSONNEL WILL ENCOUNTER THESE RATIOS IN DUN AND BRADSTREET REPORTS, AND FINANCIAL STATEMENTS PROVIDED BY SUPPLIES IN ADDITION TO ANNUAL REPORTS.
- <u>INVENTORY TURNOVER</u> INDICATES THE APPROXIMATE NUMBER OF TIMES THE AVERAGE STOCK OF INVENTORY WAS SOLD AND REPLENISHED DURING THE PERIOD (NORMALLY ONE YEAR)

$$\text{INVENTORY TURNOVER} = \frac{\text{COST OF GOODS SOLD}}{\text{AVERAGE INVENTORY}}$$

$$= \frac{\$6,085}{(\$1,703 + \$1,439)/2}$$

$$= 3.87 \text{ TIMES}$$

- **DAYS RECEIVABLE OUTSTANDING – NEXT TO CASH AND MARKETABLE SECURITIES, RECEIVABLES ARE THE MOST LIQUID ASSETS. THEY CAN OFTEN BE CONVERTED RIGHT INTO CASH. THIS RATIO MEASURES THE NUMBER OF DAYS, ON AVERAGE, IT TOOK TO GENERATE THE SALES UNCOLLECTED AT YEAR END. IT IS COMPUTED AS ENDING RECEIVABLES DIVIDED BY AVERAGE DAILY SALES.**

$$\text{DAYS RECEIVABLE OUTSTANDING} = \frac{\text{ENDING RECEIVABLES}}{\text{AVERAGE DAILY SALES}}$$

$$= \frac{\$1,678}{\$9,734/365} = 62.9 \text{ DAYS}$$

- **DEBT TO EQUITY RATIO – MOST BUSINESS ENTERPRISES HAVE TWO BASIS SOURCES OF CAPITAL – DEBT AND EQUITY. CREDITORS REGARD EQUITY AS A CUSHION AGAINST FUTURE OPERATING LOSSES AND BANKRUPTCY. THE LARGER THE % OF TOTAL ASSETS FINANCED BY EQUITY CAPITAL, THE MORE SECURE ARE THE CREDITORS. AGGRESSIVE GROWTH ORIENTED ORGANIZATIONS TEND TO RELY MORE HEAVILY**

ON DEBT THAN EQUITY, WHEREAS STABLE, CONSERVATIVE ORGANIZATIONS TEND TO HAVE A LARGER PROPORTION OF EQUITY.

DEBT TO EQUITY RATIO = $\dfrac{\text{TOTAL LIABILITIES}}{\text{TOTAL STOCKHOLDER EQUITY}}$ = 0.74

THE RATIO OF 0.74 INDICATES THAT THE CREDITORS HAVE PROVIDED $0.74 OF CAPITAL FOR EACH $1.00 PROVIDED BY STOCKHOLDERS. STATED ANOTHER WAY, FOR EACH $1.74 OF ASSET BOOK VALUES, THE COMPANY COULD SUFFER A $1.00 LOSS AND STILL HAVE TOTAL ASSETS ON THE BOOKS EQUAL TO TOTAL LIABILITIES.

- **TIMES INTEREST EARNED, A MEASURE OF INTEREST PAYING ABILITY, WHICH SHOWS THE RELATIONSHIP BETWEEN EARNINGS AVAILABLE TO PAY INTEREST AND TOTAL INTEREST EXPENSE.**

$$\text{TIMES INTEREST EARNED} = \frac{\text{NET INCOME} + \text{INTEREST EXPENSE} + \text{INCOME TAXES}}{\text{INTEREST EXPENSE}}$$

$$= \frac{\$951 + \$345 + 811}{\$345}$$

$$= 6.11 \text{ TIMES}$$

- **CURRENT RATIO MEASURES THE RELATIONSHIP BETWEEN CURRENT ASSETS AND CURRENT LIABILITIES**

$$\text{CURRENT RATIO} = \frac{\text{CURRENT ASSETS}}{\text{CURRENT LIABILITIES}}$$

$$= \frac{\$5,246}{\$2,248} \qquad = 2.33$$

NOTE: THE HIGHER THE RATIO, THE STRONGER THE COMPANY.

- **QUICK RATIO SHOWS AMOUNT OF CASH, SECURITIES AND RECEIVABLES THAT CAN BE OBTAINED RELATIVELY QUICKLY FOR EACH $1.00 OF CURRENT LIABILITIES OUTSTANDING. ANALYSTS CONSIDER A RATIO OF 1.0 TO BE ADEQUATE FOR MOST BUSINESSES.**

$$\text{QUICK RATIO} = \frac{\text{MARKETABLE CURRENT}}{\text{CURRENT LIABILITIES}}\text{CASH + SECURITIES +RECEIVABLES}$$

$$= \frac{\$1,335 + \$250 + \$1,678}{\$2,248} = 1.45$$

- **THE ASSET TURNOVER RATIO MEASURES THE ABILITY OF THE FIRM TO USE ASSETS TO GENERATE SALES. IT IS COMPUTED AS SALES DIVIDED BY AVERAGE TOTAL ASSETS.**

$$\text{ASSET TURNOVER} = \frac{\text{SALES}}{\text{AVERAGE TOTAL ASSETS}}$$

$$= \frac{\$9,734}{(\$8.754 + \$7,555)/2}$$

$$= 1.19 \text{ TIMES}$$

NOTE: DUN AND BRADSTREET (D+B) CAN BE OF GREAT IMPORTANCE, ESPECIALLY WHEN NEGOTIATING WITH A NEW SUPPLIER OR WHEN UPDATING THE STATUS OF A SUPPLIER. FOR A FEW, D+B CAN PROVIDE IMPORTANT INFORMATION ON MOST COMPANIES.

CHAPTER TWENTY-TWO

SAMPLE CLOSINGS

- "DO YOU WANT THE SOFA DELIVERED MONDAY OR TUESDAY?"
- "WOULD YOU PREFER THE STANDARD OR THE UPGRADED MODEL?"
- "DO YOU WANT TO CHARGE IT OR PAY CASH?"
- "DID YOU SAY YOU WANT 100 WIDGETS OR 10?"
- "OUR PRICES ARE GOING UP TOMORROW. IF YOU WANT TO LOCK IN A LOW PRICE, YOU'D BETTER ACT NOW!"
- "YOU KNOW, THERE WAS ANOTHER BUYER HERE THIS MORNING. HE SAID HE WOULD PROBABLY COME BACK TOMORROW."

CHAPTER TWENTY-THREE

BUYER'S REMORSE
REAL OR IMAGINARY?

- **SOONER OR LATER, WE MAKE BAD PROCUREMENT DECISIONS**
  - WE PAID TOO MUCH, OR PRODUCT DID NOT LIVE UP TO EXPECTATIONS
- **CHECK COMPETITION!! ONLY WAY TO DETERMINE IF YOU PAID TOO MUCH**
  - OVERPAYMENT WAS SMALL – DISREGARD
  - IF OVERPAYMENT WAS LARGE, RETURN OR VISIT THE RETAILER, WHO OFTEN WILL ADJUST PRICE IF YOU ASK
- **WHAT IF YOU CANNOT AFFORD TO PAY FOR IT?**
  - DOES THE STATE HAVE A "COOL DOWN" LAW? SOME RETAILERS DO
- **IF STUCK WITH THE ITEM, CONSIDER THE FOLLOWING:**
  - IF PRESSURED INTO SALE BY SLICK CAMPAIGN, SEE ATTORNEY IMMEDIATELY
  - MANY PURCHASES CAN BE RESCINDED BY FILING A SMALL CLAIMS ACTION, OR LAWSUIT ALLEGING SALE WAS THE RESULT OF FRAUDULENT MISREPRESENTATION OF FACTS
  - CAN YOU NEGOTIATE A PAYMENT SCHEDULE THAT YOU AND SALESMAN CAN LIVE WITH?
  - YOU MAY WANT TO RE-SELL THE ITEM TO CUT YOUR LOSS – IF YOU FIND NO OTHER ALTERNATIVE

CHAPTER TWENTY-FOUR

BUDGETING WHILE NEGOTIATING TIME

- **BUDGETING DOES NOT NORMALLY REFER TO THE TRADITIONAL MONETARY BUDGETING PROCESS**
- **ADDRESSES TIME, ENERGY, MONEY, EMOTIONS – KEEP ON TOP OF REAL PRICE**
- **BUDGET FORMULA**
  - TIME = VALUE x

  - ENERGY = VALUE 2x

  - MONEY = VALUE 3x

  - EMOTION = VALUE 4x

- **WHICH OF THE FOUR ITEMS ABOVE IS MOST IMPORTANT TO YOU? WHY?**
- **KNOW ADVERSARY'S BUDGET**
- **KEEP YOUR MONETARY BUDGET AS LOW AS POSSIBLE**
- **INCREASE ADVERSARY'S TIME BUDGET – "TIME INTENSIFIES PAIN"**
  - MAKE THEM WAIT – AFTER ALL, THIS IS YOUR TIME

  - GIVE SHORT NOTICE FOR MEETING, ESPECIALLY IF ADVERSARY MUST TRAVEL A LONG DISTANCE (ONE DAY IF COMING FROM CALIFORNIA TO NORTH CAROLINA SHOULD BE ENOUGH)

- FLOOD THEM WITH EMAIL TRAFFIC AND FAXES, EVEN PHONE CALLS

- LAST MINUTE CANCELLATION OF MEETINGS, OR RESCHEDULE

- UNEXPECTED CHANGE IN AGENDA WILL KEEP ADVERSARY OFF HIS FEET, AND ABSORB MORE OF HIS TIME

- CONTINUE TO DO YOUR REGULAR BUSINESS, EVEN WHEN YOUR ADVERSARY IS AT THE TABLE

- DELAY COMPLETION OF MEETING BY SEARCHING FOR MAKE BELIEVE ASSISTANCE FROM MAKE BELIEVE PERSON

- **ASKING QUESTIONS THAT DO NO GOOD IS A WASTE OF BUDGETED TIME**
- **MAKING ASSUMPTIONS WITHOUT DOING RESEARCH IS A WASTE OF TIME**
- **LAZINESS IS A TERRIBLE WASTE OF TIME. ACTUALLY, MOST NEGOTIATORS DO A TERRIBLE JOB RESEARCH AND/OR PREPARING FOR NEGOTIATING SESSIONS. DO YOUR RESEARCH!! DON'T WORRY ABOUT YOUR OPPONENT**
- **KNOW WHO "CALLS THE SHOTS" TO AVOID WASTE OF TIME, ENERGY AND MONEY**

CHAPTER TWENTY-FIVE

THE THREE CRITICAL ELEMENTS

TIME, INFORMATION, POWER

- **<u>TIME</u>**
    - TIME CAN BE YOUR GREATEST FRIEND OR GREATEST ENEMY

    - NORMALLY, 80% OF NEGOTIATING RESULTS ARE ACHIEVED IN 20% OF THE ALLOCATED TIME (PARETO RULE)

    - HAVE PATIENCE
        - SINCE MOST SETTLEMENTS OCCUR IN THE LAST FEW MINUTES, WAIT FOR THE RIGHT MOMENT TO ACT

    - BE PERSISTENT
        - IF YOUR FIRST APPROACH DOES NOT WORK, TRY ANOTHER. PATIENCE AND PERSISTENCE PAY OFF IN NEGOTIATING

    - MOVE QUICKLY WHEN POSSIBLE AND APPROPRIATE. SOMETIMES, YOUR OPPONENT NEEDS TO BE CONVINCED ON THE BENEFITS TO HIM OF A SPEEDY NEGOTIATION

    - REALIZE DEADLINES CAN BE CHANGED
        - DON'T PANIC – YOU CAN CHANGE THE DATE!

    - KNOW YOUR OPPONENT'S TIME LINE

- ▪ DON'T REVEAL YOUR TIME LINE
- ▪ OPPONENT'S PANIC LEVEL WILL INCREASE AS YOU APPROACH HIS/HER TIME LINE

- ▪ MAKE TIME WORK FOR YOU
  - ▪ MOVE SLOW AND WITH PERSEVERANCE

• <u>INFORMATION</u>

- ▪ THE SIDE WITH THE MOST AND BEST INFORMATION USUALLY COMES OUT FIRST IN NEGOTIATIONS
  - ▪ WHY DO PEOPLE OFTEN GO INTO NEGOTIATING SESSIONS WITH INADEQUATE INFORMATION?
  - ▪ WHY DO YOU GO TO SEVERAL DEALERSHIPS BEFORE BUYING A CAR?

• <u>POWER</u>

- ▪ POWER HAS HAD A BAD CONNOTATION FOR MANY YEARS

- ▪ LET'S REDEFINE POWER AS THE ABILITY TO INFLUENCE PEOPLE OR SITUATIONS

- ▪ IT IS THE ABUSE OF POWER THAT IS BAD

- ▪ SEVERAL TYPES OF POWER CAN INFLUENCE THE OUTCOME OF A NEGOTIATION SESSION. SOME OF THE PRIMARY TYPES ARE LISTED BELOW:
  - ▪ SOME MEASURE OF POWER IS CONFERRED BASED ON ONE'S FORMAL POSITION IN THE ORGANIZATION

- SOME PEOPLE HAVE KNOWLEDGE AND INFLUENCE. IT IS THE USE OF THESE ELEMENTS THAT CONFERS POWER.

- THE MORE TRUSTWORTHY NEGOTIATORS ARE, THE MORE POWER THEY HAVE IN NEGOTIATING

- PEOPLE WHO ARE ABLE TO BESTOW REWARDS HOLD POWER. MONEY HAS POWER, BUT ONLY IF IT IS DISTRIBUTED

- THOSE WHO HAVE THE ABILITY TO CREATE NEGATIVE OUTCOME FOR AN OPPONENT HAVE THE POWER TO PUNISH

- DEALING WITH AN OPPONENT OF THE OPPOSITE SEX CAN CONFER POWER. DOES A WOMAN CREATE POWER WHEN SHE REACHES OVER THE TOUCHES THE OPPONENT ON THE LEG? YOU DECIDE

- WHAT DID JOHN F. KENNEDY, MOTHER TERESA AND RONALD REAGAN HAVE IN COMMON? HOW ABOUT PASSION AND CONFIDENCE IN WHAT THEY BELIEVED IN?

- THE SIDE WITH THE LEAST INTEREST IN THE NEGOTIATING SESSION HOLDS THE GREATEST POWER. DO YOU HAVE AN EXAMPLE?

NOTE: THERE IS A LINK BETWEEN A NEGOTIATOR'S SELF-ESTEEM AND THE AMOUNT OF POWER THAT A PERSON BELIEVES HE OR SHE HAS. NEGOTIATORS WITH HIGH SELF-ESTEEM FEEL THEY HAVE MORE VIABLE OPTIONS, AND THUS MORE POWER TO ACT. THE REVERSE IS TRUE WITH A NEGOTIATOR WITH LOW SELF-ESTEEM

LET'S DISCUSS SOME ASSOCIATED ASPECTS OF POWER IN NEGOTIATING

- SOME NEGOTIATORS TRY A POWERFUL TACTIC WITH THEIR OPPONENT, "I DO NOT EVEN NEED YOU OR WHAT YOU HAVE TO OFFER. I CAN DO BUSINESS WITH ANOTHER COMPANY." THIS IS A TOUGH SHARK-LIKE MANEUVER THAT MAKES INEXPERIENCED NEGOTIATORS FEEL POWERLESS. HOW TO YOU RESPOND TO THIS "TIGER?" ASK THIS QUESTION – "IF YOU DO NOT NEED THAT I OFFER, WHY DID YOU AGREE TO MEET WITH ME?" ASKING POWERFUL QUESTIONS IS THE ONLY WAY TO DETERMINE JUST HOW MUCH POWER YOU DO HAVE.
- INCIDENTALLY, POWER EXISTS ONLY TO THE POINT AT WHICH IT IS ACCEPTED

CHAPTER TWENTY-SIX

STRATEGIC QUESTIONING,

ACTIVE LISTENING
- **START WITH A VERB INTERROGATIVE**
- **VERBALIZED IS JUST THAT – QUESTION BEGINS WITH A VERB**
  - CAN YOU DO THIS?

  - IS THIS YOUR EXPECTATION?

  - WHAT RESPONSE SHOULD YOU ANTICIPATE FROM VERB-LED QUESTION?

- **AVOID QUESTIONS THAT MAKE YOUR ADVERSARY UNCOMFORTABLE**
  - OPEN-ENDED QUESTION – "WHAT WOULD YOU LIKE FOR ME TO DO?"
    - PUTS ADVERSARY AT EASE

    - HAS NO REASON TO FEAR YOU

- **WHO HAS CONTROL OVER THE CONVERSATION – THE PERSON LISTENING OR THE PERSON SPEAKING?**
  - THE _____ DOES. LET YOUR ADVERSARY DO THE TALKING.

  - WHICH QUESTIONS ARE BEST – THOSE LED BY A VERB OR THOSE LED BY AN INTERROGATIVE?

- THOSE QUESTIONS LED BY "WHO," "WHERE," "WHEN," "WHY," "WHICH," "HOW," "WHAT" SEEK INFORMATION FROM YOUR ADVERSARY

- THE GOOD NEGOTIATOR MASTERS THE ART OF OPEN-ENDED AND INTERROGATIVE LED QUESTIONS

- <u>PARTICIPANTS</u> – IDENTIFY SOME QUESTIONS FROM EACH OF THE TWO CATEGORIES

- KEEP QUESTIONS ON THE SHORT SIDE – 9 TO 10 WORDS

- LOOK FOR NON-VERBAL EXPRESSIONS FROM YOUR ADVERSARY
    - <u>PARTICIPANTS</u> – IDENTIFY OBSERVATIONAL "CLUES" AND EXPLAIN WHY THEY ARE IMPORTANT

- LEARN TO LISTEN ACTIVELY BY <u>PARAPHRASING</u> WHAT YOUR ADVERSARY SAYS
    - "MR. SMITH, IF I HEARD YOU CORRECTLY, YOU HOPE TO ACHIEVE _____"
    - PARAPHRASING ALLOWS YOU TO GET INFORMATION RIGHT THE FIRST TIME

- ACTIVE LISTENING BUILDS IMMEDIATE SUPPORT
    - BE OPEN AND RECEPTIVE WITH YOUR BODY LANGUAGE (GIVE EXAMPLE)
    - HEAR ALL YOUR ADVERSARY SAYS BEFORE RESPONDING
    - DON'T INTERRUPT OR FINISH A SENTENCE

- LISTEN FOR FEELINGS EXPRESSED BY YOUR ADVERSARY

- WHERE DO YOU WANT TO SPEND AS MUCH TIME AS POSSIBLE?
  - IN YOUR _____ WORLD
  - ALLOWS NEGOTIATOR TO SEE WHAT ADVERSARY SEES

SILENCE IS GOLDEN

- **SILENCE IS AN EFFECTIVE TECHNIQUE WHEN NEGOTIATING WITH SOMEONE WHO CANNOT SHUT UP**
  - DON'T BE AFRAID TO LET THE OTHER SIDE DOMINATE THE CONVERSATION

- **THE BEST NEGOTIATORS ARE THOSE WHO REGULARLY ASK THE OTHER SIDE OPEN-ENDED QUESTIONS**
- **IF OTHER SIDE WANTS TO SAY SOMETHING, DON'T INTERRUPT!!**

CHAPTER TWENTY-SEVEN

NONVERBAL COMMUNICATION

- **DOMINANCE AND POWER**
  - PLACE FEET ON DESK
  - MAKING PIERCING EYE CONTACT
  - PUTTING HANDS BEHIND HEAD
  - PLACING HANDS ON HIPS
  - GIVING A PALM-DOWN HANDSHAKE
  - STANDING WHILE COUNTERPART IS SEATED
  - FINGERTIPS TOUCHING

- **DISAGREEMENT, ANGER, SKEPTICISM**
  - RED IN THE FACE
  - CROSSING ARMS AND LEGS
  - SQUINTING
  - FROWNING
  - TURNING BODY AWAY

- **UNCERTAINTY, INDECISION**
    - CLEANING GLASSES
    - LOOKING PUZZLED
    - FINGERS IN MOUTH
    - BITING LIP
    - PACING
    - TILTED HEAD

- **EVALUATION**
    - NODDING
    - TILTING HEAD SLIGHTLY
    - STROKING CHIN
    - HANDS ON CHEST
    - INDEX FINGERS TO LIPS
    - MAINTAINING GOOD EYE CONTACT

- **SUBMISSION, NERVOUSNESS**
    - FIDGETING
    - MINIMUM EYE CONTACT
    - TOUCHING HANDS TO FACE, HAIR

- USING BRIEFCASE TO "GUARD" BODY

- GIVING PALM-UP HANDSHAKE

- CLEARING THROAT

- **BOREDOM, LACK OF INTEREST**
  - FAILING TO MAKE EYE CONTACT

  - PLAYING WITH OBJECTS ON DESK

  - STARING BLANKLY

  - DRUMMING ON TABLE

  - PICKING AT CLOTHES

  - LOOKING AT WATCH, DOOR

- **SUSPICION, DISHONESTY**
  - TOUCHING NOSE WHILE SPEAKING

  - COVERING MOUTH

  - AVOIDING EYE CONTACT

  - USING INCONGRUOUS GESTURES

  - MOVING BODY AWAY

- **CONFIDENCE, COOPERATION, HONESTY**
  - LEANING FORWARD

  - ARMS AND PALMS OPEN

  - GREAT EYE CONTACT

  - FEET FLAT ON FLOOR

  - LEGS UNCROSSED

  - SMILING

CHAPTER TWENTY-EIGHT

NEGOTIATING TACTICS - VARIOUS

- THE <u>BUYER</u> IS PURCHASING A NEW COMPUTER. "IS $999 YOUR BEST PRICE?"

  <u>COMPUTER SALESMAN</u>: "THIS COMPUTER WILL GO FOR $850 IN ONE WEEK. LET ME ASK AND SEE IF THE MANAGER WILL APPROVE THE SALES PRICE FOR YOU TODAY"

  SIMPLY BY ASKING, THE BUYER SAVED #149!!

- WHEN TRYING TO WIN A CONCESSION OR GAIN A POINT IN A NEGOTIATION, ASKING A CLOSED-ENDED QUESTION IS A GOOD IDEA. CLOSED-ENDED QUESTIONS ARE EFFECTIVE BECAUSE THEY ARE DIRECT AND TO THE POINT

  <u>BUYER</u>: IF I CAN GET MANAGERIAL APPROVAL FOR TWO NEW TOOLS, WHICH WOULD NORMALLY INCUR A COMBINED COST OF $15,500, CAN YOU GET THE PRICE UNDER $14,000?

- <u>OPEN-ENDED QUESTIONS</u> ALMOST ALWAYS START WITH <u>WHO, WHAT, WHEN, HOW OR WHY</u>. THEY PERMIT THE NEGOTIATOR TO OBTAIN AS MUCH ACCURATE INFORMATION AS POSSIBLE

EXAMPLE: IN PURCHASING A USED CAR, THE BUYER IS INTERESTED IN THE FREQUENCY OF OIL CHANGES. SHE DECIDES AGAINST THE QUESTION, "HAVE YOU CHANGED THE OIL FREQUENTLY?" IN FAVOR OF, "TELL ME WHAT TYPE OF MAINTENANCE HAS BEEN DONE ON THIS CAR."

- IF YOU ARE GOING TO CONCEDE IN THE OPENING ROUNDS OF A NEGOTIATION SESSION, <u>CONCEDE SMALL</u>!!

EXAMPLE: YOU ARE SELLING YOUR RIDING LAWN MOWER/TRACTOR FOR $1,900. YOUR FIRST OFFER IS $1,600. INSTEAD OF COUNTERING WITH A LOWER NUMBER LIKE $1,750 IN THE FIRST ROUND, TRY COUNTERING WITH A LARGER AMOUNT, LIKE $1,850. THE LARGER AMOUNT IS NORMALLY A BETTER STARTING POINT

- MOST LIKELY, YOU HAVE BEEN CAUGHT UP IN THE <u>GOOD GUY, BAD GUY</u> SITUATION

EXAMPLE: THE CAR SALESPERSON SAYS HE CANNOT APPROVE YOUR OFFER WITHOUT FIRST TAKING IT TO THE SALES MANAGER FOR REVIEW. UPON RETURN, THE SALESPERSON SAYS THE "DEAL IS CLOSE" BUT THE OFFER WILL NOT WORK

SUGGESTION: EXPOSE THE TECHNIQUE. TELL THE SALESPERSON THAT IF HE DOES NOT

HAVE THE <u>AUTHORITY</u> TO MAKE THE DEAL, HE SHOULD BRING IN SOMEONE WHO DOES. WARN HIM – THE NEXT TIME HE LEAVES THE ROOM, YOU LEAVE ALSO

- <u>THE "SWEET" CARPET DEAL</u> – THE CUSTOMER TELLS THE SALESPERSON, "YOUR CARPET IS $1.00 PER YARD MORE EXPENSIVE THAN YOUR COMPETITOR'S." THE SELLER "SWEETENS" THE DEAL BY SAYING, "I WILL CARPET YOUR CLOSETS FOR FREE IF YOU SIGN THE CONTRACT TODAY"

- <u>THE TRADE – OFF CONCESSION</u> MIGHT WORK AT THIS POINT. THE CUSTOMER SAYS, "I WILL SIGN THE CONTRACT TODAY IF YOU CARPET THE CLOSETS FOR FREE AND HAVE THE CARPET INSTALLED BY FRIDAY"

CHAPTER TWENTY-NINE

LEARNING HIGHLIGHTS

- A FEW KEY IMPORTANT HIGHLIGHTS FROM THIS MATERIAL ARE DETAILED BELOW. THESE GO HAND-IN-HAND WITH ALL OTHER ASPECTS TO
    - MEASURABLY INCREASE YOUR KNOWLEDGE OF NEGOTIATING STRATEGIES
    - BETTER PREPARE YOU FOR THE "TIGERS" THAT WILL CONFRONT YOU ACROSS THE TABLE. THESE "MANEATERS," SO TO SPEAK, TAKE NO PRISONERS!! THEY ARE NOT YOUR FRIENDS. GIVE THEM REASON TO RESPECT YOUR KNOWLEDGE AND DETERMINATION AND WINNABILITY.

- THE POPULAR TERM, "WIN-WIN" CAN BE HARMFUL. STATED ANOTHER WAY, THE TERM EQUALS "COMPROMISE."
    - COMPROMISE CANNOT BE GOOD, BECAUSE YOU ARE LIKELY GIVING UP SOMETHING
    - THE ECONOMIC HEALTH OF ANY FIRM IS IN NO SMALL PART RELATED TO BUYER PERFORMANCE AND KNOWLEDGE, AND WILLINGNESS TO BECOME "INUNDATED" IN THE MANY TECHNIQUES CONTAINED HEREIN. COMPROMISE IS ONE KEY WAY TO DENY ECONOMIC HEALTH, AS YOU WILL SEE

- THE "TIGER" ACROSS THE TABLE HAS SHARP TEETH AND A MASSIVE APPETITE. HE/SHE IS, IN FACT, YOUR ADVERSARY, NEVER YOUR FRIEND

- YOU CAN CALL HIM/HER YOUR "RESPECTED OPPONENT," IF "ADVERSARY" BOTHERS YOU

- **ALMOST ALL NEGOTIATING DECISIONS ARE EMOTION-BASED, NOT DECISION-BASED. EMOTIONALLY-BASED NEGOTIATING PLAYS ON YOUR HEART STRINGS**
  - KEEP YOUR EYE FOCUSED ON THE OBJECTIVE, NOT WHETHER YOU WIN

- **SUCCESS SOMETIMES MEANS WALKING AWAY WITH A POLITE "GOODBYE."**

- **YOUR ADVERSARY USES A DEVICE WITH A HIGH-POWER TELESCOPIC LENS – YOU ARE THE TARGET**

- **UNDERSTAND THE GREATEST WEAKNESS OF ALL - NEEDINESS**

  - THE MOMENT YOU EXPRESS NEED, YOU'VE LOST CONTROL

  - TIGERS ARE EXPERTS IN RECOGNIZING NEED – AND

  - IN CREATING NEED

- **ALSO NOTE THAT "YES" AND "MAYBE" ARE INCONCLUSIVE**

  - THE JAPANESE WILL DRIVE YOU CRAZY WITH "MAYBE" – WHAT DOES IT REALLY MEAN" TIE IT DOWN!!

- SAYING "NO" SHOULD NOT BOTHER YOU – IT CLEARING DEFINES YOUR POSITION

- **MANY NEGOTIATORS WANT TO BE LIKED – IT WILL LEAD TO TROUBLE FOR YOU!!**

  - DON'T SAVE THE ADVERSARY OR SAVE THE RELATIONSHIP. DON'T FEAR HURTING FEELINGS

- **GET INFORMATION BY ASKING QUESTIONS – DO NOT GIVE INFORMATION!**

CHAPTER THIRTY

B A T N A -(BEST ALTERNATIVE TO A NEGOTIATED AGREEMENT)

- BEFORE ENTERING THE NEGOTIATING ROOM, CONSIDER WHAT ALTERNATIVE(S) WILL BE ACCEPTABLE IF YOUR NEGOTIATION BREAKS DOWN
- EXAMPLE: IF NEGOTIATIONS "SO SOUTH," HAVE YOU ALREADY IDENTIFIED ANOTHER VIABLE OPPONENT (COMPETITOR)?
- A REAL, VIABLE ALTERNATIVE ALMOST ALWAYS STRENGTHENS YOUR NEGOTIATING POSITION.
- SOMETIMES, ANGER SETS IN, TENSIONS RUN HIGH, AND REACHING A SOLUTION BECOMES IMPOSSIBLE, OR SO IT SEEMS
- BREAKING A DEADLOCK IS POSSIBLE, AND USUALLY DESIRABLE
- ASK OPEN-ENDED QUESTIONS
- LISTEN ACTIVELY – INACTIVE LISTENING DOES NOT ALLOW COMMON GROUND
- AVOID GETTING PERSONAL – FOCUS ON THE ISSUES
- DON'T GET STUCK ON PRESERVING YOUR OWN INTERESTS
- RESTART WITH SMALL DEAL POINTS AND WORK TOWARDS "YES" GRADUALLY
- IS ANOTHER ALTERNATIVE BEST FOR BOTH PARTIES?
- STOP, TAKE A BREAK, AND AGREE ON RESTART TIME

CHAPTER THIRTY-ONE

TESTING THEIR LIMITS

- **ASK FOR A DISCOUNT FOR CASH**
  - SEEK DISCOUNT AFTER DEAL IS SETTLED
  - MANY SUPPLIERS WILL DECLINE REQUEST FOR DISCOUNT
  - GENERALLY, SEEK 2% - 5%
  - SOME BUSINESSES HAVE REASON FOR ACCEPTING CASH – THEY DO NOT REPORT ON THEIR INCOME TAX
- **COMMUNICATE FINALITY**
  - MAKE THEM BELIEVE YOU HAVE REACHED YOUR LIMIT, OR
  - USE DEADLINE PRESSURE TO IMPLY FINALITY, AND
  - PUSH UNTIL THEY PUSH BACK
  - ABRUPT FINALITY CAN BE COUNTERPRODUCTIVE – FORCES OPPONENT TO CONCESSIONS OR SURRENDER
  - AVOID COMMUNICATING SUCH EXTREME FINALITY THAT OPPONENT LOSES FACE
  - TIME YOUR MOVE CAREFULLY – COMMUNICATING FINALITY WHEN YOU ARE FAR APART CAN RESULT IN DEADLOCK
- **LET THEM SAVE FACE THROUGH YOUR MANNER/ WORDS**
  - CONSIDER MAKING FINAL CONCESSION, LEAVING SOMETHING ON THE TABLE
  - AVOID PERSONAL ATTACKS AND REMARKS – CAN BE COSTLY
  - IF YOU WIN, ACT GRACIOUSLY
  - DON'T GLOAT

- SOONER OR LATER, YOU MAY MEET AGAIN, SO DON'T BURN THE LAST BRIDGE!!
- **PICK UP LOOSE CHANGE – OPPONENT MAY OTHERWISE TAKE MONEY "LEFT ON THE TABLE"**
- **TEST YOUR ASSUMPTIONS – TEST YOUR OPPONENT'S LIMITS BY PUSHING FURTHER THAN YOU DO ON ALL WORTHWHILE ITEMS**
- **LOOK FOR SIGNS OF TACIT ACCEPTANCE AND THEN TEST THEM**
  - "IT LOOKS LIKE WE CAN WORK SOMETHING OUT"
  - NOT SAYING "NO" OFTEN MEANS "YES"
- **IF OPPONENT IS UNYIELDING, GENTLY THREATEN TO BREAK OFF NEGOTIATIONS**
- **WATCH FOR SIGNS YOU HAVE GONE TOO FAR**
  - LISTEN CAREFULLY
  - BALANCE PUSHING WITH DELICACY AND SENSITIVITY
  - BACK OFF QUICKLY IF THEY ARE READY TO BLOW UP
  - ACCEPTING THEIR LAST OFFER MAY BE MORE IMPORTANT THAN FACING DEFEAT
- **BREAK BEFORE CLOSING THE DEAL**
  - CHECK EVERY IMPORTANT ISSUE
  - MAKE SURE BOTH SIDES HAVE SAME UNDERSTANDING
  - WAIT UNTIL FINAL MOMENT IF YOU WANT TO "SLIP" SOMETHING PAST THE OPPONENT

CHAPTER THIRTY-TWO

BEHAVIOR WHILE NEGOTIATING
WHAT IS YOUR STYLE?
(YOU SELECT BEST RESPONSE)

- **IN PREPARATION FOR NEGOTIATING, YOU**
  - A. ___ WONDER WHAT YOUR OPPONENT WILL BE LIKE AND HOPE YOU WILL NOT BE TAKEN ADVANTAGE OF
  - B. ____ MENTALLY PREPARE TO COMPETE WITH YOUR OPPONENT AND BEGIN TO PLAN YOUR STRATEGY
  - C. ____ CAUTIOUSLY PREPARE YOUR CASE, MAKING SURE YOU HAVE SUPPORTING DATA AND RESEARCH TO SUPPORT YOUR POSITION
- **WHEN INITIALLY MEETING YOUR COUNTERPART, YOU**
  - A. ___ TAKE TIME TO CONNECT ON A PERSONAL LEVEL AND CONCERN YOURSELF WITH SETTING A POSITIVE TONE
  - B. _____ PUSH TO QUICKLY PRESENT YOUR GOALS, FACTS, AND DATA, HAVING LITTLE TIME FOR SOCIAL FORMALITIES
  - C. __ BEGIN THE PROCESS SLOWLY, LISTENING TO YOUR COUNTERPART'S POSITION BEFORE PRESENTING YOUR INFORMATION
- **IN PRESENTING INFORMATION DURING THE NEGOTIATION, YOU**
  - A. ____ WANT TO MAKE SURE YOUR COUNTERPART KNOWS YOUR CONCERN, BUT ALSO KNOWS THAT YOU ARE CONCERNED WITH THEIR POSITION

- B. _____ PRESENT ONLY INFORMATION THAT WILL STRENGTHEN YOUR POSITION
- C. ___ HAVE A STRONG NEED TO PRESENT ALL FACTUAL INFORMATION IN A DETAILED, SEQUENTIAL AND COMPLETE MANNER

- **WHEN IT IS DIFFICULT TO GAIN AGREEMENT ON A POINT, YOU ARE LIKELY TO**
  - A. _____ COMPROMISE YOUR POSITION IF IT MEANS YOU CAN OBTAIN AGREEMENT AND PRESERVE THE RELATIONSHIP
  - B. _____ KEEP PURSUING YOUR OPTIONS UNTIL YOU GAIN WHAT YOU WANT
  - C. _____ ASK QUESTIONS TO FURTHER UNDERSTAND YOUR COUNTERPART'S POSITION, WHILE CONTINUING TO PRESENT FACTS TO SUPPORT YOUR POSITION

- **WHEN YOUR COUNTERPART SURPRISES YOU WITH IMPORTANT INFORMATION YOU DID NOT HAVE, YOU**
  - A. ___ FEEL THAT YOUR TRUST HAS BEEN VIOLATED
  - B. ___ QUICKLY COUNTER ASSERTIVELY WITH NEW INFORMATION OF YOUR OWN
  - C. _____ EXAMINE THE NEW INFORMATION IN CLOSE DETAIL

- **IN TRYING TO REACH AN OUTCOME, AT TIMES YOU**
  - A. ___ LET THE OTHER PARTY DETERMINE THE OUTCOME FOR THE SAKE OF REACHING AGREEMENT
  - B. _____ USE THE OTHER PARTY'S WEAKNESS TO YOUR ADVANTAGE
  - C. ___ HAVE NOT BUDGED FROM YOUR POSITION IF YOU FELT THAT YOU WERE RIGHT AND THE OTHER PARTY WAS NOT BEING ETHICAL

- **DURING THE NEGOTIATION, YOUR COMMUNICATION WITH THE OTHER PARTY**
  - A. _____ IS INFORMAL AND NOT ALWAYS RELATED SPECIFICALLY TO THE NEGOTIATION
  - B. _____ IS ASSERTIVE, DIRECT AND SPECIFIC TO THE NEGOTIATION
  - C. ___ IS CAUTIOUS, RESERVED AND UNEMOTIONAL
- **WHEN A NEGOTIATION IS NOT GOING WELL FOR YOU, YOU**
  - A. ___ GET FRUSTRATED AND BEGIN TO FEEL YOU ARE BEING PERSONALLY TAKEN ADVANTAGE OF
  - B. ___ FOCUS ON STRATEGIES YOU CAN USE TO ACHIEVE YOUR DESIRED OUTCOME
  - C. ___ FOCUS ON THE AVAILABLE FACTS AND DATA AND LOOK FOR VIABLE ALTERNATIVES TO HELP YOU ACHIEVE YOUR DESIRED OUTCOME
- **WHEN YOU NEED ADDITIONAL INFORMATION FROM YOUR COUNTERPART, YOU**
  - A. _____ WORRY THAT YOUR COUNTERPART WILL FEEL PRESSURED OR THREATENED BY TOO MANY QUESTIONS
  - B. _____ QUESTION YOUR COUNTERPART DIRECTLY, TARGETING ONLY SPECIFIC INFORMATION YOU NEED TO BE SUCCESSFUL
  - C. ___ QUESTION YOUR COUNTERPART THOROUGHLY TO ENSURE THE FACTS YOU HAVE ARE COMPLETE AND DETAILED
- **AT THE CONCLUSION OF THE NEGOTIATION, YOU**
  - A. __ CARE ABOUT WHAT YOUR COUNTERPART THINKS ABOUT YOU AND TRY HARD TO END THE NEGOTIATION ON A POSITIVE NOTE
  - B. _____ ARE LESS CONCERNED ABOUT WHAT YOUR COUNTERPART THINKS ABOUT YOU AND MORE

CONCERNED ABOUT WHETHER YOU HAVE ACHIEVED YOUR GOALS

- C. __ ARE CONCERNED THAT YOUR COUNTERPART FEELS THE FINAL OUTCOME WAS FAIR

    A. __ TOTAL
    B. __ TOTAL
    C. __ TOTAL
    GRAND TOTAL ____

CHAPTER THIRTY-THREE

THE NEGOTIATING ATMOSPHERE

- **A FRIENDLY ATMOSPHERE IS USEFUL IN MANY NEGOTIATIONS**
    - WHEN SOLVING JOINT PROBLEMS
    - WHEN IN A WEAK BARGAINING POSITION
        - THE WEAKER YOU ARE, THE LESS EMPHASIS YOU WANT ON POWER
        - "NO THANKS" TO COFFEE CAN HELP TURN AN ADVERSARY INTO A POTENTIAL FRIEND
    - A SERIOUS RISH CAN OCCUR FROM BEING TOO FRIENDLY
        - CAN CREATE DISTRUST
        - FRIENDLINESS CAN CREATE NATURAL SUSPICIONS
    - SOME PEOPLE, PARTICULARLY DOMINANT ONES, VIEW FRIENDLINESS AS A SIGN OF WEAKNESS
- **THE FORMAL ATMOSPHERE IS SOMETIMES APPROPRIATE, SUCH AS**
    - WHEN UNSURE OF WHAT TO DO
    - WHEN DEALING WITH DETACHED PEOPLE
    - WHEN PARTIES ARE HOSTILE TO EACH OTHER
    - WHEN ISSUES ARE COMPLEX
- **INDIFFERENT ATMOSPHERE – CAN BE IN YOUR FAVOR**
    - OTHER SIDE MAY MAKE CONCESSIONS BECAUSE YOU SEEM NOT TO CARE ABOUT REACHING A GOAL
    - YOU CREATE THIS ATMOSPHERE BY BEING COLD, EVEN HOSTILE

- YOU CAN BLUFF – BUT BE A GOOD ACTOR!!
- YOU MUST BE CONVINCING
- YOU RUN RISK OF DEADLOCK

- ## **HOSTILE ATMOSPHERE**
  - CREATE BY BEING HOSTILE
  - APPLIES WHEN OTHER SIDE TAKES AN OUTRAGEOUS POSITION
    - MAKE SURE THEY UNDERSTAND YOUR ANGER
    - CREATE <u>ONLY</u> WHEN ABSOLUTELY NECESSARY

  - THIS CAN CREATE RESISTANCE OR EVEN REFUSAL TO DO BUSINESS WITH YOU

CHAPTER THIRTY-FOUR

PLAY TIME

- <u>OBJECTIVE</u>: NEGOTIATING SESSION BETWEEN SALESPERSON, JOHN BROWN, AND PURCHASING MANAGER, DAVE WHITE, TO DISCUSS SALE OF A NEW DRILLING MACHINE.
- <u>DAVE</u>: (LEAVES JOHN BROWN IN THE LOBBY FOR 35 MINUTES AS HE ATTENDS TO OTHER BUSINESS).
- <u>DAVE</u>: GOES TO LOBBY TO MEET THE SALESPERSON, AND ESCORTS JOHN TO A WOOD CHAIR WITH NO CUSHIONS. MEANWHILE, DAVE HAS A SEAT IN HIS LARGE, OVERSTUFFED CHAIR BEHIND HIS DESK. DAVE LIGHTS UP A CIGARETTE, AND CALLS HIS SECRETARY TO BRING ONE CUP OF COFFEE TO THE OFFICE.
- <u>DAVE</u>: "JOHN, THANKS FOR STOPPING BY TODAY. SORRY, BUT I ONLY HAVE 10 MINUTES – GOT ANOTHER SALESPERSON COMING IN FROM GREENSBORO. INCIDENTALLY, THANKS FOR FLYING OUT TO SEE ME WITH SUCH SHORT NOTICE. HOW WAS YOUR TRIP FROM SAN DIEGO?"
- <u>JOHN</u>: I HAD A THUNDERSTORM OVER ST. LOUIS, WHICH CAUSED ME TO MISS MY CONNECTING FLIGHT IN CHARLOTTE, WHERE I HAD A SEVEN HOUR LAYOVER. AVIS GAVE AWAY MY CAR IN RALEIGH, SO I HAD TO TAKE A TAXI OUT TO YOUR PLANT. I HOPED YOU COULD JOIN ME FOR LUNCH – I HAVEN'T EATEN SINCE YESTERDAY

MORNING WITH ALL THE PROBLEMS GETTING HERE, BUT IT SOUNDS LIKE YOU ARE GOING TO BE TIED UP LATER."

- (PHONE RINGS – DAVE SAID, "EXCUSE ME, JOHN," AND HE THEN ANSWERED THE PHONE – THE CALL WAS CONCLUDED ABOUT SEVEN MINUTES LATER)

- <u>DAVE</u>: "SORRY JOHN, I HAD TO TAKE THAT CALL. MY WIFE WANTED TO TELL ME ABOUT HER TENNIS LESSONS. NOW, WHY DON'T YOU PROCEED?"

- <u>JOHN</u>: "DAVE, I'M GLAD YOU COULD SEE ME. MY COMPANY IS ANXIOUS TO DO BUSINESS WITH YOUR COMPANY. I HAD DINNER WITH YOUR SENIOR EQUIPMENT ENGINEER LAST MONTH. HE TOLD ME YOU ARE INTERESTED IN PURCHASING A NEW BITING MODEL XYZ DRILLING MACHINE. HE ALSO TOLD ME MY QUOTE OF $155,000 WAS VERY ATTRACTIVE. HE INFORMED ME OF THE LACK OF WARRANTY SUPPORT ON THE OTHER BITING TOOL YOU PURCHASED LAST YEAR FROM MY COMPETITOR. I REALIZE YOU CAN BUY ANOTHER BITING TOOL FROM THE SAME SUPPLIER, BUT I CAN ASSURE YOU OF THE VERY BEST WARRANTY SERVICE IN THE INDUSTRY. WE CAN BE HERE WITHIN FIVE DAYS IF YOUR TOOL BREAKS DOWN. AND, MY LEAD TIME FOR THE NEW TOOL IS ONLY NINE WEEKS, WHICH WOULD MEET YOUR NEEDS, ACCORDING TO YOUR ENGINEER. FRANKLY, YOU WILL HAVE VERY FEW PROBLEMS WITH THIS YEAR'S MODEL – IT HAS BEEN UPDATED

TO FIX THE MOTOR THAT REPEATEDLY BURNED OUT."

- (PHONE RINGS AGAIN. DAVE PICKED UP THE HANDSET. AFTER CONCLUDING THE CALL, DAVE SAID:

- <u>DAVE</u>: "JOHN, I APOLOGIZE ONCE AGAIN. THAT WAS THE SALESPERSON COMING IN FROM GREENSBORO AFTER YOU LEAVE. SEEMS WE ARE GOING TO THE GOVERNOR'S INN FOR LUNCH. NOW, BACK TO YOUR PROPOSAL. YES, JOHN, YOU ARE CORRECT. WE DO NEED TO PURCHASE ANOTHER BITING DRILLING MACHINE, BUT FRANKLY, I HAVE SOME RESERVATIONS THAT SHOULD BE ADDRESSED. YOU SEE, OUR BUDGET FALLS SHORT OF YOUR QUOTE. WE ONLY HAVE $120,000 FOR THIS PURCHASE. YOUR COMPETITOR SAID HE CAN MEET OUR BUDGETED NUMBER. ALSO, HE PROMISED TO DELIVER IN ONLY FOUR WEEKS, AND SIGN A PENALTY STATEMENT THAT WOULD APPLY IF HE MISSES THE PROMISED DELIVERY DATE. WE HAVE A GOOD TRACK RECORD WITH YOUR COMPETITOR, AND HE DELIVERED THE TOOL WE PURCHASED LAST YEAR ON TIME. ALSO, HE OFFERED TO EXTEND THE WARRANTY FROM 12 TO 15 MONTHS AT NO EXTRA EXPENSE, AND GIVE US TERMS OF 3% 10, NET 30. FRANKLY, I AM RELUCTANT TO GO WITH A DIFFERENT SUPPLIER. I REALLY DO NOT BELIEVE ANYONE CAN EQUAL THE OFFER THEY MADE. JOHN, THANKS FOR MAKING THE TRIP TO VISIT WITH ME. I AM SORRY WE CANNOT DO ANY

BUSINESS. PLEASE HAVE A SAFE JOURNEY BACK TO CALIFORNIA."
- <u>JOHN</u>: "THANKS, DAVE, FOR YOUR TIME"

- <u>CONCLUSION</u>
- WHAT ARE YOUR OBSERVATIONS ON HOW DAVE HANDLED THIS MEETING? WAS HE RUDE, OR IS THAT TO BE EXPECTED IN A NEGOTIATING SESSION?
- ANY NOTEWORTHY EVENTS STAND OUT FOR DISCUSSION?
- WHAT OPTIONS DOES JOHN HAVE, IF ANY? DID HE DO ANY RESEARCH BEFORE MAKING THE TRIP?
- COULD JOHN DO ANYTHING UP FRONT TO AVOID THE WASTED TRIP?
- DID DAVE DO RESEARCH BEFORE HE MET WITH JOHN?
- DID DAVE PLAN HIS STRATEGY FOR THIS MEETING?
- WAS DAVE BEING FACTUAL IN HIS DISCUSSION WITH JOHN? HOW DO YOU KNOW?
- WAS "SMALL TALK" EXCHANGED BETWEEN THE TWO? WHAT IS THE PURPOSE OF "SMALL TALK?"
- WOULD YOU CONSIDER DAVE A "POWER NEGOTIATOR?" WHY? WHAT IS A POWER NEGOTIATOR?
- WHY DID DAVE LEAVE JOHN IN THE LOBBY FOR 35 MINUTES? WAS DAVE'S POSITION STRENGTHENED?
- WHAT WAS THE POSSIBILITY OF A DEADLOCK IN THIS MEETING? WHAT IS A "WALKOUT?"

- **FACTS TO CONSIDER:**
- **JOHN'S COMPANY HAS A DEMO TOOL THAT COULD BE OFFERED TO DAVE (IT IS THE CURRENT MODEL, AND IS OPERATIONAL). JOHN'S PROFIT MARGIN ON THE DEMO MACHINE IS 44%. JOHN'S COMPETITOR IS IN FINANCIAL TROUBLE, AND RECENTLY DECIDED TO CEASE OPERATION. WAS DAVE AWARE OF THIS MATTER? SHOULD IT BE CONSIDERED BY DAVE? WHY DID HE NOT NEGOTIATE WITH JOHN?**

CHAPTER THIRTY-FIVE – SECTION A

GENERAL INFORMATION ON CAR PURCHASE

- **DETERMINE WHAT YOU WANT TO BUY**
- **SEE "A PLAN FOR CAR PURCHASE" ON SEPARATE SHEET**
  - TAKE THE "BASE PRICE" OF THE CAR AND ADD THAT "BASE PRICE" OF THE OPTION PACKAGE YOU WANT.
    - THE "DEALER'S COST" OR INVOICE AMOUNT IS SET FORTH IN EDMUND'S CATALOGUE OR CONSUMER REPORTS, AVAILABLE AT BOOKSTORE OR LIBRARY.

  - SUBTRACT FROM IT ALL REBATES OFFERED BY THE MANUFACTURER AND THE DEALER. THE RESULT IS THE "OFF THE LOT PRICE" AND WHAT YOU SHOULD PAY.
    - TO DETERMINE WHAT THE REBATES ARE, CALL THE DEALERSHIP YOU ARE GOING TO WORK WITH

    - INFORM THE SALESPERSON OF YOUR INTENDED PURCHASE – SPECIFY CAR YOU ARE SEEKING, INCLUDING MODEL NUMBER. TELL THEM WHERE YOU LIVE, AND THAT YOU HAVE AN OFFER TO BUY THIS VEHICLE AT (RESEARCH PRICE), BUT YOU CAN'T GET IT IN THE DESIRED COLOR (WHITE). IF HE/SHE HAS THE CAR IN THIS COLOR, YOU WILL BUY IT FROM THEM. IF NOT, YOU WILL BUY THE OTHER CAR IN YOUR AREA.

- SPECIFY THE PRICING CONTAINED IN "THE PLAN FOR CAR PURCHASE."

- IT IS NOT PRACTICAL FOR THE DEALER TO TELL YOU TO COME TO THEIR OFFICE TO NEGOTIATE. THEY ARE PUT IN UNCOMFORTABLE POSITION OF ACCEPTING OR REJECTING YOUR OFFER.

- AFTER THEY AGREE, FAX CONFIRMING LETTER (SEE "A PLAN FOR CAR PURCHASE")

CHAPTER THIRTY-FIVE – SECTION B

POWER IN PURCHASING A CAR

- **BUYERS GENERALLY HATE CAR DEALERS, WITH GOOD REASONS. IT IS IMPORTANT TO UNDERSTAND HOW THEY VIEW THE SALE.**
- **GOOD CAR DEALERS WILL GIVE SPACE TO THE BUYER – BUT GOOD DEALERS ARE RARE!!**
    - "LOOK FIRST . . . THEN I'LL MAKE YOU A GREAT DEAL!!"
- **SELECT THE CAR YOU WANT – DEALER CONGRATULATES YOU AND MOVES TO THE "BONDING" EXPERIENCE**
    - "TAKE THE CAR HOME WITH YOU TONIGHT. LOOK AT THE GADGETS, SUSPENSION, ALL THE FINE FEATURES." YOU THINK THE DEALER IS NOT SUCH A BAD GUY AFTER ALL!!

- **NOW, LET'S GET DOWN TO BUSINESS:**
    - SMILE!! WHEN PLEASANT AND POSITIVE, YOU APPEAR CONFIDENT. SMILING IS A CHEAP CONCESSION – LOWERS ADVERSARY'S SHIELD
    - USE FIRST NAME – PEOPLE LIKE TO BE CALLED BY THEIR FIRST NAME. FORMALITY MEANS ARM'S LENGTH NEGOTIATIONS.
    - EASE INTO NEGOTIATIONS – RELAX, DISCUSS ANYTHING TO BREAK THE ICE AND HELP YOUR ADVERSARY TO ALSO RELAX.

- BE OPTIMISTIC – AT LEAST ACT LIKE YOU ARE!! OPTIMISM CAUSED ADVERSARY TO VISUALIZE A SUCCESSFUL DEAL.

- USE CONFIDENCE-BUILDING GESTURES. SHOW INTEREST IN CONCERNS AND INTERESTS OF THE OTHER SIDE.

- SEARCH FOR COMMON GROUND BEFORE DIFFERENCES – RELIGIOUS, POLITICAL, SOCIAL, AWARENESS OF ISSUES THAT ARE EASILY RESOLVED.

- STATE ADVERSARY'S POSITION BETTER THAN THEY CAN – EVEN IF YOU DISAGREE. ADVERSARY IS MORE LIKELY TO LISTEN TO YOUR VIEW WHEN THEY BELIEVE YOU UNDERSTAND THEIRS.

- SEEK PRIVACY AWAY FROM OPEN EARS WHEN DISCUSSING DISPUTES WITH YOUR COMPANION.

- HELP ADVERSARY SAVE FACE – WHEN WE LOSE FACE, WE GENERALLY RETALIATE. LOOK FOR WAYS YOUR ADVERSARY CAN SELL THE DEAL.

CHAPTER THIRTY-FIVE – SECTION C

WHEN TO BUY A CAR

- **NEVER BUY A NEW CAR IN A RURAL AREA OR A SMALL TOWN**
    - TYPICALLY, THE AVERAGE DEALERSHIP'S OVERHEAD PER VEHICLE IS LOWER IN LARGER CITIES.

    - THERE IS A LARGER POOL OF CARS FOR EACH DEALERSHIP THAN THERE IS IN A LESSER POPULATION AREA.

    - MOST CAR DEALERSHIPS IN SMALLER AREAS TEND TO HAVE A HIGHER FIXED OVERHEAD THAN IN MORE DENSELY POPULATED AREAS.

- **BUY A NEW CAR BETWEEN JUNE AND AUGUST**
    - CAR DEALERS ARE FACED WITH CLASSIC CASH SQUEEZE DURING THIS PERIOD

    - REQUIRED TO PURCHASE NEXT YEAR'S MODELS, OR ARRANGE CASH DOWN

    - APPROXIMATELY THREE MONTHS BEFORE NEW MODELS HIT SHOWROOM, VALUE OF EXISTING MODELS BEGIN TO DEPRECIATE – OFTEN DRAMATIC DROP

    - DEALERSHIP'S LINE OF CREDIT WITH BANKS IS COLLATERALIZED BY THIS INVENTORY

- BANKS OFTEN DEMAND DEALERSHIP POST ADDITIONAL CASH

- COVERS THE SHORTFALL (COMPENSATING BALANCES")

- DEALERSHIPS OFTEN WILLING TO SELL CARS FOR SIGNIFICANTLY LESS TO GENERATE CASH FLOW

- SALESPERSONS OFTEN GIVEN "BONUSES FOR UNITS SOLD"

- DEALERSHIPS MAY INTRODUCE OTHER BUYER INCENTIVES

CHAPTER THIRTY-FIVE – SECTION D

A PLAN FOR CAR PURCHASE

- **BASE PRICE (CAR)** $29,500
- **BASE PRICE (OPTIONS)** $3,100
- **DEALER'S COST (INVOICE) (SEE NOTE 1)** $32,600
- **REBATES/OFFERS (SUBTRACT) (SEE NOTE 2)** $1,500
- **OFF THE LOT PRICE (SEE NOTE 3)** $31,100

  NOTE 1: SEE EDMUND'S CATALOGUE OR CONSUMER REPORTS AT LIBRARY OR BOOKSTORE

  NOTE 2: OBTAIN OVER THE PHONE

  NOTE 3: AMOUNT YOU PAY INCLUDES TAX, LICENSE FEE, ETC.

- **FINALLY, CALL THE DEALER. AFTER THE OFFER IS ACCEPTED, FAX DEALER THE FOLLOWING LETTER.**

James A. Smith

ABC CAR COMPANY   APRIL 15, 2014

THIS IS TO CONFIRM OUR AGREEMENT OF TODAY WHEREIN YOU AGREED TO SELL ME THE 2014 ACURA RT/XL, COLOR WHITE, OPTION PACKAGE XYZ, FOR THE FOLLOWING "OFF THE LOT" PRICE (TAXES, LICENSE FEES INCLUDED) FOR $31,100.

I WILL BRING A CASHIER'S CHECK WITH ME TOMORROW FOR THIS AMOUNT. PLEASE SIGN IN THE SPACE PROVIDED BELOW TO CONFIRM OUR UNDERSTANDING OF THIS AGREEMENT, AND FAX THIS DOCUMENT TO 919-555-5555.

I AGREE TO THE FOREGOING

_____

NAME OF DEALER

NOTE: THIS IS NOT A LEGAL DOCUMENT. SEE YOUR ATTORNEY IF NECESSARY.

CHAPTER THIRTY-SIX

NEGOTIATING WITH OTHER CULTURES

- **THE AMERICAN WAY TO NEGOTIATE IS DIFFERENT FROM APPROACHES FOUND IN EVERY OTHER COUNTRY**
- **CERTAIN VALUES AFFECT OUR NEGOTIATING APPROACHES**
  - TIME – AMERICANS ARE SLAVES TO THE CLOCK
    - TREATED AS VALUABLE RESOURCE
    - ARRIVING EARLY AT NEGOTIATING SESSIONS SUGGESTS WE ARE ANXIOUS AND SERIOUS
    - ARRIVING LATE SAYS WE ARE NOT CONCERNED OR INTERESTED
  - SPACE IS ALSO HIGHLY REGARDED, CONTRARY TO VIEWS IN MOST OTHER CULTURES
    - IN AMERICA, SITTING NEAR AN OFFICE WINDOW IS OFTEN VIEWED AS RECOGNITION OF HIGHER STATUS
    - IN JAPAN, SITTING NEAR A WINDOW REFERS TO EMPLOYEES BEING RETIRED
  - IN AMERICA, A SMALL OFFICE IS OFTEN A REFLECTION OF LOWER STATUS

- IN SOUTH AMERICA OR ARAB COUNTRIES, THE OPPOSITE IS TRUE

- IN AMERICA, HARD WORK WILL USUALLY BE REWARDED
  - SELF-DETERMINATION IS A CONCEPT ALMOST OUTSIDE THE COMPREHENSION OF MANY OTHER CULTURES

- STRIVING IN THE AMERICAN SENSE IS UNCOMMON IN SOUTHEAST ASIA
  - BUDDHISTS BELIEVE THAT SUFFERING IS CAUSED BY DESIRE FOR POSSESSIONS

- MANY CULTURES VIEW AMERICANS AS "WORKAHOLICS"
  - IN MOST OTHER CULTURES, WORK IS GENERALLY SOMETHING THAT MUST BE DONE OUT OF NECESSITY, CERTAINLY NOT APPRECIATION FOR ITS OWN SAKE

- PEOPLE FROM THE MIDDLE EAST OFTEN TOUCH OR HOLD HANDS
  - CAN YOU IMAGINE AMERICANS DOING THIS?

- AMERICANS BELIEVE LOOKING DIRECTLY INTO ANOTHER PERSON'S EYES IS A SIGN OF HONESTY
  - THE JAPANESE VIEW THIS ACTION AS RUDE

- AMERICANS ASSUME OUR OPPONENT UNDERSTANDS US WHEN HE NODS HIS HEAD

- ▪ JAPANESE MAY COMPLETELY DISAGREE WHEN HE NODS HIS HEAD – IT ONLY MEANS HE IS TRYING TO UNDERSTAND US

- RUSSIANS REGARD NEGOTIATIONS AS DEBATES
- IN JAPANESE AND ARAB COUNTRIES, NEGOTIATIONS ARE OFTEN COMBINED WITH SOCIAL ACTIVITIES
- JAPANESE NEGOTIATING TEAMS WILL NOT INCLUDE YOUNG "HOT SHOTS" (AS WE OFTEN DO IN AMERICA)
- BE CAREFUL OF DISCUSSIONS ON RACISM OR SEXISM
  - ▪ ONE WAY JAPAN PROVIDES FOR JOB SECURITY FOR MEN IS TO PROVIDE ALMOST NO JOB SECURITY TO WOMEN
  - ▪ NEARLY ALL FEMALES ARE ON SHORT-TERM CONTRACTS
  - ▪ IN SOME ARAB COUNTRIES, WOMEN ARE NOT ALLOWED TO DRIVE, TO WALK ALONE, AND THEY RUN THE RISK OF BEING ARRESTED FOR PROSTITUTION

- **RECOMMENDATIONS – IF YOU ARE NEGOTIATING**
  - DEMONSTRATE RESPECT FOR THE CULTURE
  - STUDY THE CULTURE BEFORE NEGOTIATING
  - DO NOT DIRECT YOUR REMARKS TO LOWER-STATUS PEOPLE
  - SLOW DOWN AND LISTEN
  - AVOID CONFRONTATIONS – AT ALL COSTS
  - ACCEPT ATTITUDES AS LEGITIMATE
  - PAY ATTENTION TO SOCIAL ASPECTS OF NEGOTIATING
  - CONSIDER USING A LOCAL PERSON AS CULTURAL ADVISOR

- NEVER ASSUME YOUR WAY IS THE ONLY WAY
- BE ABSOLUTELY CERTAIN BEFORE YOU WRITE OR SIGN A CONTRACT
  - LOCAL COURTS MAY INTERPRET YOUR AGREEMENT IN WAYS YOU NEVER IMAGINED
  - IF POSSIBLE, CONSULT A LOCAL ATTORNEY

- BE VERY CAREFUL OF CORRUPTION!!
- WHEN YOU ARE HANDED A BUSINESS CARD, TAKE TIME TO READ IT. ALSO, LOOK AT REVERSE WHICH MIGHT CONTAIN IMPORTANT INFORMATION. NEVER PLACE THE BUSINESS CARD IN YOUR POCKET WITHOUT FIRST READING IT.

CHAPTER THIRTY-SEVEN

AGENDA – IMPORTANCE AND DEVELOPMENT

- **AGENDAS HELP BUILD EMOTIONAL CONTROL**
- **TROUBLE PREPARING AGENDAS MEANS TROUBLE WITH GOALS, M & P, ETC.**
- **EVEN A PHONE CALL OR EMAIL, NO MATTER HOW SHORT, REQUIRES AN AGENDA**
- **AGENDA CAN CONTAIN:**
  - NAME/PHONE NUMBER OF CONTACT
  - PROBLEMS
  - REFERENCES TO PAST TOPICS
  - THEIR BAGGAGE
  - OUR BAGGAGE
  - WHAT WE WANT/DON'T WANT
  - WHAT HAPPENS NEXT

CHAPTER THIRTY-EIGHT

MANAGING TIME

- **WHEN NEGOTIATING, TIME CAN BE YOUR BEST FRIEND**
    - USE TO YOUR ADVANTAGE
    - STALL AND STALL AND STALL UNTIL OTHER SIDE GIVES UP
    - IF ONE SIDE IS UNDER PRESSURE, THE OTHER SIDE HAS THE DISTINCT ADVANTAGE
    - IF NEGOTIATING WITH PROCRASTINATORS, CREATE VISIBLE AND TIGHT DEADLINES
    - UNBALANCED PRESSURE OCCURS IF YOU MUST RUSH TO THE AIRPORT OR GO TO AN OTHER MEETING

CHAPTER THIRTY-NINE

CULTURAL COMPARISONS

LATIN AMERICA

PREPARATION:	POOR
DECISION-MAKING:	INDIVIDUALIST
PROTOCOLS AND RULES:	NONE
ARGUMENTS:	NO LIES, BUT WILL MAKE IT UP
RELATIONSHIPS:	INFORMAL, IMPORTANT
RISK-TAKING:	HIGH TO MEDIUM
FLEXIBILITY:	HIGH TO CREATIVE
TIME VALUE:	LOW
STYLE:	EMOTIONAL/PASSIONATE
AGREEMENTS:	MODERATELY IMPORTANT

JAPANESE

PREPARATION:	HIGH AND INTENSE
DECISION-MAKING:	CONSENSUS, MULTIPLE REVIEWS
PROTOCOLS AND RULES:	EMPHASIZED
ARGUMENTS:	BASED ON DETAILED STUDIES
RELATIONSHIPS:	TRUSTWORTHY, FACE-SAVING
RISK-TAKING:	LOW
FLEXIBILITY:	VERY LITTLE
TIME VALUE:	RELATIVELY LOW
STYLE:	FORMAL
AGREEMENTS:	DOCUMENTED IN MINUTES

WESTERN EUROPEAN-FRENCH

PREPARATION:	MOERATE
DECISION-MAKING:	INDIVIDUALIST
PROTOCOLS AND RULES:	HIGHLY VALUED
ARGUMENTS:	BASED ON LOGIC, REASON
RELATIONSHIPS:	BUSINESS FIRST
RISK-TAKING:	MEDIUM TO LOW
FLEXIBILITY:	CONTROLLED
TIME VALUE:	HIGH (MUCH LIKE USA)
STYLE:	NATIONALISTIC
AGREEMENTS:	ORALLY WITH CONTRACTS LATER

MIDDLE EAST-ARABIC

PREPARATION:	ABSURD INITIALLY
DECISION-MAKING:	INDIVIDUALIST
PROTOCOLS AND RULES:	EMPHASIZED
ARGUMENTS:	BASED ON POWER, POLITICS
RELATIONSHIPS:	PRAISE FOR HOSPITALITY
RISK-TAKING:	VERY HIGH
FLEXIBILITY:	MODERATE TO LOW
TIME VALUE:	LOW
STYLE:	INTERRUPTED ENVIRONMENT
AGREEMENTS:	WORD BASED

EASTERN EUROPEAN-RUSSIAN

PREPARATION:	**GENERALLY HIGH**
DECISION-MAKING:	**COLLECTIVE**
PROTOCOLS AND RULES:	**IMPORTANT**
ARGUMENTS:	**PERSISTENT**
RELATIONSHIPS:	**FORMAL**
RISK-TAKING:	**MEDIUM**
FLEXIBILITY:	**VERY BUREAUCRATIC**
TIME VALUE:	**LOW**
STYLE:	**CRITICAL ATTITUDE**
AGREEMENTS:	**COMPLIANCE WITH THE SPIRIT OR INTENT**

D & B REPORTS

DO YOU WANT TO DETERMINE THE FINANCIAL HEALTH OF A NEW SUPPLIER, OR TO ASCERTAIN THE GENERAL CONDITION OF A SPECIFIC COMPANY, THEN INITIATE A D&B (DUN & BRADSTREET) REPORT REQUEST. PLEASE SEE THE ATTACHED SAMPLE OF INFORMATION GENERALLY AVAILABLE FROM D&B FOR A NOMINAL FEE.

D+B SUPPLIER EVALUATION REPORT

- **SPECIAL EVENTS**
- **FINANCIAL PROFILE**
- **OPERATION**
- **HISTORY**

Printed in the United States
By Bookmasters